**You've got this:
How to continue your freelance career
when you become a mother**

Dorota Pawlak

Copyright © 2020 by Dorota Pawlak

All rights reserved.

No part of this book may be reproduced in any form of by any other electronic or mechanical means, except in the case of brief quotations embodied in articles or reviews—without written permission from its author.

This book provides the most accurate information possible. Many of the strategies, methods, and tips come from personal experiences. The author shall not be held liable for any damages resulting from use of this book.

Editor: Susan Gaigher

Cover design: Yassine Arrahil

Pictures on the cover: Freepik

ISBN: 9798682577415

Contents

Introduction	4
FREE GIFT	7
PART 1: Interviews	8
Viki Stelma-Boviatsis	10
Laura Innocenti	16
Isis Nyong'o	22
Maha AlBisher	26
Kateryna Vinitskyi-Sikoza	31
Sandra Duquenne	38
Anna Kamay	42
Ambika Gupta	47
Mariana Ciocca Alves Passos	54
Cyville Harriette F. Jaum	60
Daniela Helguera	63
Christy Racho	69
Anastasia Shnyper	74
Rachel Reiter	78
Magdalena Stojer-Brudnicka	83
PART 2: Reflections	96
Before the Revolution	98
Getting ready for the unexpected	99
The burden of the first year	108
The financial meanders	118
Slowing down won't slow you down	121

Getting used to the new order 127
   Where is my mind? 131
   Where is my time? 137
   What if I'm losing it? 149
   Is there anyone else? 153
   How can I stay on top of it? 163
   What if there's a cloud on the horizon? 169
   Where shall I go? 177
When new opportunities arise 180
   Thriving in your business 181
   Lifelong learning 185
   Giving up is freeing up 190
Bibliography 196
Photography credits 199
Found a typo? 200
About Dorota Pawlak 201
Acknowledgements 203
One last thing 204

Introduction

It takes a village to raise a mother. But it probably takes two, if the mother is self-employed.

The life of a first-time mother is full of challenges, surprises, sacrifices, unexpected emotions, uncontrolled tears, and laughter. The life of a mother who runs her own business can be even more intense on each and every level. Lack of security tied to full-time salaried employment, limited or almost non-existent maternity leave, doubts about how to keep both your customers and your family happy, combined with high costs of childcare may all be reasons for a constant headache and emotional roller coaster long before the child is born.

How can you prepare for this new lifestyle? Is it actually possible to combine freelance work with motherhood, especially with no family support or limited access to childcare? Is moving your work to the late-night hours the only way out? How can you make sure you'll have enough energy to meet the needs of your (fussy) baby and your (picky) customers?

There's no one reasonable answer to all these questions. But there's a large dose of inspiration and motivation to be gained from the experiences of other self-employed mothers. This book gathers stories of 15 women from across the world who work in various industries. Their approaches to business and motherhood might differ, as well as their definition of "success", "good childcare", or "work-family balance". But they all have an important lesson to share.

Of course, what worked for me or any of the interviewed women may not work for you. Every family, every child, and every situation is different. Child benefits, welfare systems, and childcare structures and support for freelancers also vary from country to country. That's why I invite you to treat the tips contained in this book not as an ultimate guide but merely as suggestions that might help you on your journey to rewarding motherhood and satisfying work. Consider our advice as a list of ingredients. Select your favourite and locally available items to create a unique meal that will fit you, your business, and your family.

FREE GIFT

I have a special gift for you. This book focuses on managing your life in a way that gives you more space for your family, yourself, and your business. One important element of this combination is choosing the right time-management method. This can be a real game-changer for every mother and business owner.

If you need more inspiration on this topic, click the link below to get my free e-book with handy tips on time management for busy freelancers.

Go to http://bit.ly/EBookByDorota to download the e-book and boost your time-management skills.

PART 1: Interviews

Nothing becomes real until it's experienced:
Stories of self-employed mothers

You can't prepare to be a mother.

No matter how many books or articles you read, no matter how many parents you talk to, no matter how many stories your mother, sister, or grandmother tells you, there's always a big surprise waiting for you on the other side. It may develop slowly in the background without you noticing anything, or it may appear suddenly and turn your world upside down. Whatever happens, no amount of reading, listening, talking, or meditating will fully set you up for your transition into motherhood. Especially if you are self-employed.

I've always had a tendency to overprepare for events and situations that mattered to me. The freelance mother's lifestyle was an exception to this rule. Although I read tons of books on pregnancy and raising children, I failed to draw up an action plan for my life as a mother and a business owner. Once my baby arrived, I had no choice but to keep improvising and learning during every single step.

I often wondered if other self-employed mothers have a magic formula for striking the right work-life balance. Are we all doomed to an endless game of juggling, sleepless nights, busy evenings, multitasking, and a constant feeling of guilt? Or maybe our new family member actually gives us so much energy, strength, and wisdom that we can easily tackle any issue that a freelancing mum may have? Is work-life balance a myth? Can we really have it all, but simply not at the same time?

Sadly, I don't have a one-size-fits-all answer to these questions. But I do have several fascinating stories that may inspire you when you decide to continue running your business with a newborn by your side.

With this in mind, I invite you to listen to 15 women from around the world—women who kept freelancing or running their businesses while taking care of their babies, with or without support from their families, with or without serious challenges, but always with some dose of excitement, gratitude, and courage.

And while no amount of listening or reading will fully prepare you for your new role, these stories may become your motivation and an effective reminder that nothing is impossible.

Viki Stelma-Boviatsis

- Co-owner of TULA Yogastudios (www.tulayogastudios.nl) with locations in Amsterdam and Ede (Netherlands)
- Half Dutch, half Greek
- Based in Amsterdam

How did your pregnancy change your work?

When I was pregnant, we had just one yoga studio and the studio was still young (two years old). The studio was open seven days a week, and daily operations continued throughout each day. We were slowly growing our business, and next to all the daily operations, I was still teaching four to six classes a week. It did not occur to me to slow down, even though I was carrying twins. I guess I was lucky that my body felt great and I did not have much physical problems during my pregnancy. I became a bit heavier in my third trimester, and this is the moment I stopped teaching yoga classes, but I never gave up all the other work which needed to be done.

How did you plan to combine your business with motherhood? Did you prepare (mentally, emotionally, financially etc.) for this new challenge before the delivery?

When I look back now, I would have slowed down much more and I would have managed my time better to fully prepare myself for motherhood. It all felt like a roller coaster.

Having just one yoga studio was challenging for us. Since our business was still young, we did not make enough money to live. So, my business partner (and husband) was still working in a wine bar three to four times a week to secure our financial situation. Mentally I knew I had to slow down and let my business partner take over, but he was also working long nights in his other job, and growing and managing a business is hard work in the beginning. I was lucky not to have any physical problems during my pregnancy.

I remember I had a huge desire to create a safe space for our boys. Back then, during my pregnancy, we lived in a 45-square-meter apartment with one bedroom which was ours, but I was worried, because we could not fit two baby cots in the bedroom, and I imagined having the babies close to me in the beginning. I was focusing on finding a new house for our family, but I also knew that it is difficult to find a house in Amsterdam. We used our entire network and asked our yoga students if they could help us. We asked via social media and via our newsletter, and we even had a poster hanging in the studio. It helped, because one of our students and her husband were moving abroad with her newborn son, and they offered us their 90-square-meter two-bedroom apartment. We moved in my second trimester, and I even helped painting the house. We were very lucky and excited because our house was just 100 meters away from TULA, so this made life much easier.

Even though my husband was still working another job as well, we were making plans on how to change our lives in a way that we could both fully commit to the studio instead of working elsewhere. Many of our students living in Amsterdam West already asked us to open another studio in Bos en Lommer, and we were making plans to fulfil this dream during my pregnancy.

What has changed in your work style after the delivery? When did you start working again?

It was just my husband and I running the business, so I started after three days after the delivery. My husband was still working in the wine bar and things needed to be done. I was lucky I could do most things from home and the boys were still sleeping many hours in the beginning. After six months, we brought the boys to a day care, and also my mother took care of them one day a week. In this first year of motherhood, we were planning to open our second yoga studio, which we did just before the boys turned one. This was the most hectic year of our lives, and I have never felt so tired, but it was such a good decision. When the second studio opened, my husband stopped his other job and we could both focus full time on the two yoga studios.

Looking back, this first year of motherhood was very intense, but our lives changed in a positive way, as opening the second studio secured our financial situation within six months.

Did you ever feel overwhelmed by stress, exhaustion, or your responsibilities as a mother of twins and a business owner? How did you cope with it?

The first year after delivery was exhausting for me. Opening a second yoga studio, managing operations, managing 50 yoga teachers and another 16 hosts next to taking care of the twins was intense. I experienced a lot of stress and I cried a lot, but my daily yoga practice was the one thing that kept me strong. I did decide not to teach any classes anymore myself, so I could focus 100% on managing the business.

Was it easy to keep your business growing when you became a mother?

I am lucky my husband is also a business owner and we both inspire each other to grow our business to the next level.

I have to admit that since I became a mother, I feel much stronger than before. I am almost like a power woman. This does not only show in the success of our business, but I feel it from inside out. In my yoga practice I feel physical, but mostly mental strength, and this brings much more balance into my personal life. This reflects on our business and results in growing our business much easier than before. Of course, you learn and grow over the years, but I feel like motherhood has a positive effect on this matter.

Was what you imagined about being a self-employed mum before the delivery different from your reality after the delivery?

Yes, I knew it would be challenging, but it made my life complete.

What was your biggest challenge and the biggest reward in your first year as a business owner and a mum?

I was doing long days (and nights) in the first year and I felt truly exhausted. Having two babies who needed lots of attention was challenging, and I could not always cope with their crying. Businesswise, we made a life-changing decision to open a second studio in this first year, which turned out to be our biggest reward, but I felt that this one year cost me five years of my life, so to speak.

Do you think that the legal and social system in the Netherlands made it easier for you to combine running your business with being a mum?

Yes, I think this is okay. I do feel day care is expensive and I can imagine that it can be challenging, especially for single working mums living in the Netherlands.

If there is one thing you would have changed to prepare better for your role as a self-employed mother, what would that be?

I would have read and studied more books about time management.

Looking back, it was not good to do work-related stuff during breastfeeding or during other moments with my babies. If I could do all of this again, I would have a 100% focus on my babies only and work on my business when I am not with them.

Can you give one important piece of advice for future self-employed mothers?

Please leave your work to rest when you are holding your child and enjoy every moment.

Laura Innocenti

- Freelance translator at www.laurainnocenti.com
- From Lucca, Italy
- Based in Recife, Brazil

How did your pregnancy change your work?

Pregnancy didn't affect my freelance work until the very end when I decided to stop working for the last month. That was mostly because my mother was going to come visit and stay with us three weeks before the due date, and I wanted to make the most of her time here. Luckily, I had a smooth pregnancy, except some heartburn at the very end, but nothing that would impact my work significantly.

I did use to teach English at a local private school the previous year. When the school shut, I immediately sent my CV to other schools. I found out I was pregnant during the interview process with one of them. At that point I didn't know whether I was going to be hired or not, but I decided not to go ahead with the hiring process as I didn't want to tackle a new work environment together with the stress of a first pregnancy in a foreign country with little support. I might have been too cautious, but I don't regret it; besides, I still had my freelance work that I could do at home at my own pace.

How did you plan to combine your self-employment with motherhood? Did you prepare for this new challenge before the delivery?

I knew from the beginning I wanted to stop working for a while postpartum, though I didn't know exactly how long. I knew that some people never really stop working, and that's great, but that was not for me. Friends kept telling me that caring for a newborn can be stressful and time-consuming, so when I stopped working, approximately one month before my due date, I warned my clients, mostly translation agencies, that I would be off work for at least three months postpartum, and that this time could be extended.

As regards finances, I knew my husband's salary could sustain us all, so that gave us some security. Additionally, I applied for a maternity check which I did obtain; it was not a lot but still a useful amount of money.

In hindsight, I am tempted to say there is nothing that can mentally and emotionally prepare you for such a huge challenge! But I did spend a lot of time during pregnancy reading about the challenges ahead. I mostly read information online and in books. I also took part in a prenatal class. I often told myself that after delivery I would have to devote at least six months of my life to taking care of my daughter full time, and that that was OK. It ended up being 10 months full time, and not being able to work for that long was frustrating at times, no matter how long I prepared mentally in advance.

What has changed in your work style after the delivery? When did you start working again?

I started working again when my daughter was 10 months old. Before that I simply didn't take on any projects. I made sure to send regular emails to my clients to let them know I was going to be on maternity leave for one, two, or three more months, or to update their online calendars as needed. I did miss working, but the deadlines are usually so tight (especially in my area, i.e. game localisation) that accepting jobs would only have made me nervous (What if I can't deliver on time? What if my daughter suddenly stops sleeping through the night?) I don't like to do a rushed, below-par job.

How did you arrange your day to be able to work and take care of your child?

When my daughter was 10 months old, I had reached the point where I could simply not continue taking care of her all day, five days a week, without losing my sanity. My husband worked full time and he did help in the evening and weekends, but that was the only help I had, as we didn't have

18

family around or friends who could help. Between hiring a nanny and a day care, we went for a day care.

We chose the times based on my freelance work. Most of my clients are European and there is a four- to five-hour difference; I must start working at around 6 am to be able to overlap with their working hours. Our daughter would therefore stay at day care from 7 am to 3 pm. That was long enough to allow me to work full time straight from the start. The only thing that changed was that I made sure not to work in the evening and at weekends, unless it was a very important project or something I really wanted to work on. At that point, I was still in charge of the evening routine for my baby, and on weekends I wanted to be able to enjoy time with my family.

How did being a mother influence your business growth and interactions with your customers?

My business hasn't grown since my daughter was born— quite the opposite, alas. I lost several good clients (agencies) during the year or so I was on maternity leave. They previously made the bulk of what I earned and sent me the most interesting jobs. Obviously, as soon as I started to work again, I refurbished my CV and sent it to dozens of potential clients as well as old clients whom I hadn't heard from in a while, but I only gained one or two new contacts, which weren't enough for me to get back to the original flow of work.

After four months of that, we had to take our daughter out of day care, as we travelled to Italy for two months and stayed at my parents' place. Straight after that we moved to a new city. My daughter still isn't back in day care as I write. Since travelling to Italy, I have only been able to take on a minimum amount of work. I only work at night and on weekends, or if someone else can help during the day, which isn't often. I admit I am not good at asking for help, so I end up accepting very little work: only small jobs with decent deadlines and a decent pay—the bare minimum in order not to lose the few good clients I have left. In order to get back to work full time I will have to enrol my daughter at a day care in our new city—hopefully soon!

What was your biggest challenge and your biggest reward in your first year as a freelancing mum?

My biggest challenge was finding time to work when I needed time to focus and my daughter wasn't at school. I had to learn to ask for help and to hire help when needed. It's hard to relinquish control when you've been the one in charge since day one. As for rewards, my first year as a mum was certainly very rewarding in many ways, but not professionally I'm afraid!

Do you think combining your self-employment with motherhood would be easier in your home country?

Not necessarily. I am not familiar with the Italian system, but as far as I know parental leave is not particularly long there, either. On a different note, my first year would certainly have been easier if I had had my mother's help for longer than five weeks.

How did you deal with unexpected situations, for example, when your child was sick and you had to work?

Luckily that has happened very rarely, but I basically finish the jobs I have started, even if it means sacrificing sleep, and stop taking on new jobs until I am positive I can handle work again.

If there is one thing you would have changed to prepare better for your role as a self-employed mother, what would that be?

I can't think of anything to be honest. As a first-time mother, it was difficult for me to predict how busy or tired I would be postpartum, despite all the advice and first-person accounts I read. In the end it's all very personal—I know of freelance mums who work while their baby sleeps on them or in a sling, but it just would not have been possible with my daughter, as during the first few months she wanted to be held for naps in a way that simply would not allow any two-handed activity! It depends a lot on the baby's routine and habits, and these vary a lot. For example, it took months before my daughter could nap in her crib during daytime, so I could never work while she napped, which is something many people do. This and other things I could simply not know beforehand. I guess freelance mums who already have one or more kids may be able to prepare better, to a certain degree at least.

Can you give one important piece of advice for future self-employed mothers?

If you can't handle it on your own, ask for help! It can be your partner, family, friends, a nanny, or day care. I completely understand wanting to take care of everything on your own, and I know it can be hard to trust someone else. But you'll find that after spending some time on your own and/or focusing on your business, you'll go back to taking care of your baby refreshed and relaxed.

Isis Nyong'o

- Owner of MumsVillage (www.mumsvillage.com)
- MumsVillage is Kenya's leading parenting website that enriches the lives of mums and mums-to-be through useful, locally relevant digital content and recently, direct access to mum and baby products via the newly launched MumsVillageShop.
- Based in Nairobi, Kenya, and originally from Michigan and Nairobi.

How did your pregnancy change your work?

I was taking a career break during my first pregnancy, and that experience inspired me to start the business I run today. I was coming out of an intense 10-year corporate stint and found that pregnancy unleashed an entrepreneurial spirit in me. Once I landed on the idea, I found that my level of creativity reached new heights.

How did you plan to combine running your business with motherhood? Did you prepare for this new challenge before the delivery?

Since I was already on a career break, I didn't prepare per se during my first pregnancy, as I was incubating the idea at the time. However, it was during my second pregnancy that I planned things out as I was establishing the business and launched it a few months before having my second child. I made sure to go to prenatal yoga weekly (despite it being an hour's drive away!) to ensure that I focused on connecting with my baby and carved out boundaries on work time when my son was born.

How did you arrange your day to be able to work and take care of your baby?

I organised my time by splitting my hours between working from home and going into the office. It wasn't an easy decision as I had a young company and a young team.

Was what you imagined about being a business owner and mum before the delivery different from your reality after the delivery?

Completely! It was much more intense than I expected, as I was constantly feeling that I wasn't adequate on either end of the spectrum. As a business owner you can't ever "switch off", and only when I was in it did I realise it would have been far more sane to be on maternity leave from a corporate job.

What was your biggest challenge and your biggest reward in your first year as a mum?

My biggest challenge was learning to give up control, especially on time—this was so hard for me. My biggest reward was traveling quite a bit when my daughter was an infant and experiencing what that was like.

Do you think the legal and social system in your country made it easier for you to combine running your business with being a mum?

Kenya has a strong pro-breastfeeding policy encouraging mums to breastfeed for six months. In addition, it's normal to breastfeed in public so I found it pretty easy to move around the city with infants.

How did the experience of being a mother change your approach to your business?

I build my schedule much more holistically than before where I had a clearer line between work and personal. Running my own business gives me a level of autonomy I would not have if I was employed, which allows for a more integrated life.

If there is one thing you would have changed to prepare better for your role as a self-employed mother, what would that be?

Overall it's a very hard thing to do—the one thing I would change looking back is to lean on my team more.

Can you give one important piece of advice for future self-employed mothers?

Try to work from home as much as you can (which is thankfully easier in the Covid and post-Covid world), especially if you're breastfeeding, to reduce the challenge around doing that well and working.

Maha AlBisher

- Owner of MB Translation (www.mbtra.com)
- From Saudi Arabia, based there as well

How did your pregnancy change your work?

The pregnancy period was all about prepping my business for my self-crafted maternity leave. I tried to finish all the big projects and didn't take on more projects to try to slow the pace before the delivery.

How did you plan to combine your self-employment with motherhood? Did you prepare for this new challenge before the delivery?

Yes, preparation is key. I gave myself a lot of grace, and I lowered my expectations. It's very important to embrace the fact that you can't do it all, nor do you have to. Being a mother is a lot of work, especially if you are a mom for the first time. As for preparing financially, I was saving up one year in advance for my maternity leave. I calculated my monthly expenses and saved up accordingly. It's very important to arrange to pay yourself during your maternity leave, even if you stopped working.

I also wrote down all the tasks in detail for my assistant, whom I hired and trained during my pregnancy. I also hired a translator and tested his skills in the areas I usually translate in. In addition to that, I talked to a couple of my colleagues and asked them if I could refer my clients to them in case we couldn't accommodate their requests.

What has changed in your work style after the delivery? When did you start working again?

I took one month off where I didn't do anything but rest and adjust to my new role as a mother, then I gradually started working again. I was fortunate enough that my assistant and my husband helped a lot during this time. My assistant would reply to all the emails and phone calls, and my husband is very familiar with my line of work, so I hired him as the project manager for a couple of important projects.

Also, I have a translator who works for me. So, he would do the work, and I would run a quality check, then my husband would take it from there.

How did you arrange your day to be able to work and take care of your child?

I work when the baby is asleep mostly. When they are little you can arrange your schedule around their nap times, but when they don't nap anymore like my three-year-old I usually allow some screen time to finish some work tasks. The trick is not having so much screen time so they don't get bored of it. Make it only for times when you need to take a break to enjoy your cup of coffee, or when you have an important conference call for instance.

How do you manage unexpected situations, for example when your child is sick and you have to work?

I ask for help. I have learned that people are willing to help when you ask for exactly what you need. I'm surrounded by a very strong support group of family. We all live close to each other. My husband is always willing to help out, and when he is not able to watch the kids, we have my mum, sister, and the in-laws. We are blessed to have this big network of support; it makes life with kids so much easier.

What was your biggest challenge and your biggest reward in your first year as a freelancing mum?

My biggest challenge was working in very limited pockets of time. I didn't have the luxury of working on a project for four to five uninterrupted hours, especially in the first months. However, I learned to be very focused and ultra-efficient with my time.

Do you think the legal and social system in your country made it easier for you to combine running your business with being a mother?

I live in Saudi Arabia and freelancing is still a relatively new concept, but our current economy is changing and lots of regulations are being changed too. So, there are many new systems that are recognising freelancing legally.

How did the experience of being a mum change your approach to your business?

I became very picky with the projects and clients I take on; not every project is worth my time and mental space. And I'm much more gentle to myself. I don't expect to do it all.

If there is one thing you would have changed to prepare better for your role as a self-employed mother, what would that be?

I would take more time off and learn to delegate more. I'm now in my second maternity leave for my second son. I'm much more relaxed, and I prioritise rest and feeling good over feeling overwhelmed.

Can you give one important piece of advice for future self-employed mothers?

Have realistic expectations about this stage of life. Know that it won't always be like this. Be intentional with your tiny bits of time. Share the load of housework and parenting with your partner, and don't apologise for it. It's your right to have a break from domestic chores and to pursue your business. Plus, I would also like to share some good resources to help mothers make the best of their time:

Books:

I know how she does it by Laura Vandercam (she studied the schedules of working moms and provides some insightful findings), *Fair Play: A Game-Changing Solution for When You Have Too Much to Do (and More Life to Live)* by Eve Rodsky.

29

YouTube Channels:

Jordan Page (she has lots of hacks for mums), Marie Forleo (she has lots of tips to grow your business).

Kateryna Vinitskyi-Sikoza

- Owner of the Singing Birds vocal studio (www.singingbirds.nl)
- Singing Birds provides vocal lessons and holds two pop choirs. It also helps to build and restore voices from scratch for singers and public speakers, especially if their voices were damaged by inadequate education, physiological problems, or mechanical injuries.
- Based in Rotterdam, the Netherlands, originally from Ukraine

How did your pregnancy change your freelance work?

I was pregnant twice, for now, and I hope for more. But let's begin from the beginning. First pregnancy was very unexpected and a huge surprise for me. I just released a solo album as singer and producer and actually had planned a promo tour across the Netherlands, also Germany, Austria, Belgium and France. When I was already three months pregnant I was presenting that album. Already at the stage of album production I had in my mind something like an internal voice: "Hey, you will release it, and will be pregnant"... and I was.

When I did the presentation, I realised that I'd have to cancel the tour. It was a very difficult decision for me because my ego was shouting "GO!", but my brain was already into motherhood mode. But I will never regret it.

I think until the sixth month of my pregnancy I was still very active with my music, just closing deals, promoting the album online, and reflecting on everything. Then I started to think about what I was going to do after delivery, as I am a person who can't live without work and be totally focused on motherhood. I wasn't ready to be an obsessive mother (no judgment and offence), who can think and live only around her children and talk only about them. I understood that I would not be able to invest a lot of time and money in my work, so I was thinking how to optimise my working hours and money flow and my music passion and the child. I finally came up with an idea that I was going to open a pop choir. Immediately I came up with the unique formula: a pop choir for expats, plus I started to give vocal lessons again. That was my life-saving belt, as a choir occurs only once per week, and five to six people could "feed" me like one performance. That income was even more stable than my performing income. Eventually, I have to say that my first pregnancy made my life totally different and my business really turned into another side and actually with lots of benefits.

With my second pregnancy, I was moving with my vocal studio and choir into a nice space. Before I did all the lessons at home, but when the choir started to grow, I had to do something about it. So, a week after my second delivery, I was painting walls, installing mirrors and acoustics in my new studio.

But during the second pregnancy I didn't have any drastic changes, maybe only in my head. I became more disciplined, started to plan all hours during the day including even going to the toilet, because keeping my business, two kids, and household in my head was just impossible. And I have to say that my husband is a priest in an Orthodox church, so he is basically only two to three evenings at home; the rest of the week he has a "normal" job and then other services in the church, so I was fully responsible for our kids and the household.

How did you plan to combine your freelance work with motherhood? Did you prepare for this new challenge before the delivery?

NO! everything was just on the flow. Yes, I was watching some videos or reading some "smart" articles, but it was with my first daughter. With the second child you are totally in a unique situation with a unique new human and in the first weeks you might be frustrated a lot. But for me everything around is just like a flow, or maybe it's a synergy with God, I would say. So, no, I was not prepared at all.

What has changed in your work style after the delivery?

I started to use my own rules and to let people go easier. For example, at the first trial lessons I tell my students: "My Dutch is not perfect, English with a heavy accent, and I teach with two kids in this room, so if you do not agree on these arrangements, you have to search for another teacher." Before having the kids, I would not have had the courage to say that. I would do everything to make the client comfortable, not myself. Obviously, I am trying to reduce uncomfortable situations for people, like engaging my older daughter with games or phone from time to time when I teach. I also give extra lessons for free, for example if the lesson is totally spoiled by my crying younger daughter or when my older daughter demands more attention. But in general, around nine out of 10 lessons go super well.

Do you think your work style has changed after you delivered the second baby?

I had to make room for more "free time" for me and the kids. That's why I optimised my schedule and work only on certain days, actually only three days a week as actual lessons and one day a week with the back office. I try to follow this schedule strictly.

Do you think combining your self-employment with motherhood would be easier in Ukraine, your home country?

Hell no! In Ukraine unfortunately people still aren't child friendly. If the family has more than three kids, they are automatically perceived as crazy, poor of mind, not well educated, etc. Even two kids are already a lot. In Ukraine only a limited number of cafes, for example, have some spaces for kids, or a kid friendly menu. Not to mention having a pumping room in the office. It's nonsense there, you would be fired as soon as your belly becomes a bit more visible than usual. So, potentially I could open the same vocal school in Kyiv, but I am not sure that I could work in the same way as in the Netherlands. Maybe I would have more help from our grannies and potentially more time for work, but then I would see my kids less often and spend less time with them. And you know, kids grow super-fast, and unfortunately, in Ukraine parents have no luxury to watch how they grow and enjoy parenting. So, thank God now I live in the Netherlands and don't have to hunt for work and money to survive. I can see how my girls are growing, developing; I play with them and combine all these things with work, which I also love.

Was what you imagined about being a freelance mum before the delivery different from your reality after the delivery?

I did not imagine anything. As I mentioned before, I live in "today" and don't think much about how things can or would be. Plus, the first pregnancy was a surprise, so I really didn't have time to think about any differences. Nine months pass so quickly when you get things done with your work, ideas, and prepare a room for your child... There was no time for imagining. The only one thing I knew for sure was that everything is possible to manage if you plan it well. And it's true. Now with the second child I even started coming back to the professional stage as a singer. It's a slow process, but I started.

What was your biggest challenge and the biggest reward in your first years as a freelancing mum?

The biggest challenge was how to stay organised and follow the plans in your calendar. It was very difficult as I used to do all tasks only when I wanted and could procrastinate a lot with difficult or boring tasks such as accounting. But with my first child I learned this skill very quickly. When you know that your child is sleeping for one hour and you know that she is a bad sleeper then you have no time for procrastination. Also, I stopped scrolling Facebook and Instagram just for fun. Now I use these two websites strictly for work purposes. I found that social media really takes so much time, and once I stopped to scroll the feed my day became three to four hours longer. So, as a reward I have to say I got the skill of super organisation and freedom from social media, and I started to talk to people more in real life, which was super difficult for me before. I used to be very shy outside of the stage and afraid of my English accent and not-perfect Dutch, but now I just don't care. I have a bit higher level of both languages at the end, just because I started to talk.

If there is one thing you would have changed to prepare better for your role as a self-employed mother, what would that be?

I think it would be a driving licence. I had a Ukrainian license, but in the Netherlands it's not valid. If I had known that travelling with the stroller with my child, with groceries and my costumes or even laptop for the lesson could be so heavy that I would end up going to a therapist to fix my back, I would have arranged for a new driving license and bought a car. Now this process has stretched into three years, just because of the short period between the first and second delivery, very limited time and more expenditures on kids' needs, not for self-education.

Can you give one important piece of advice for future self-employed mothers?

First of all, love yourself. If you love yourself, you can say to your partner: "Let's share the household chores." It looks like it's nothing, but it "eats" so much time and energy. I got burnout and then my husband got scared and immediately took over half of our household tasks. If you love yourself, you will buy a car and save your back, hands, and full body from many unpleasant things. If you love yourself, you will hire, at least once a month, a nanny and go to a spa or cafe with your friend, just to refresh your mind and get some dose of good vibes. Kids give us a lot of smiles and good emotions, but we also need a friendly talk and delicious coffee or tea outside. If you love yourself, you don't worry how you look like, because you can find the time to go shopping. If you love yourself, you can let go of some of your clients easily, because you don't have to earn so much; your mind and soul balance have to be more important than money. And eventually if you love yourself, kids love themselves and you as well. Your children need a smiling, well-balanced mum and a good example to follow, because you probably already know, you can't teach kids, you can only give examples. So, love yourself. It's not an ego thing, it's just the way to survive with your kids, your household chores, your work, and your partner.

Sandra Duquenne

- Translator and interpreter
- Based in Phnom Penh (Cambodia)
- From France
- Her children grew up in France, in Nicaragua, and Cambodia

How did your pregnancy change your work?

I wasn't as efficient as before. I had to take a nap in the afternoon for example.

How did you plan to combine your self-employment with motherhood? Did you prepare for this new challenge before the delivery?

I had been working as self-employed for 10 years and I loved it. I didn't want to change my job for a baby. Moreover, I thought that being self-employed would allow me to spend time with my baby. And I was right!

What has changed in your work style after the delivery? When did you start working again?

I started working again one week after the delivery. The baby slept a lot at the beginning, then less of course. I remember breastfeeding and typing at the same time, the baby on my lap! When she fell asleep, I had to stop typing (translating) and concentrate on the screen (revising).

How did you arrange your day to be able to work and take care of your child?

That was the hardest part, as you never know when the baby will sleep, within a minute or within an hour, if she would be brave or cry for hours because of a new tooth or be sick and have to go to the doctor... I stopped working for urgent jobs and took long-time jobs instead to be able to get better organised.

Was what you imagined about being a freelance mum before the delivery different from your reality after the delivery?

Yes! I thought that I would always be there, which I was... physically speaking... but mentally speaking, you can ask them: "Mum is always home but she's working ALL the time!" I am not as available as I thought I would be.

What was your biggest challenge and your biggest reward in your first year as a freelancing mum?

My biggest challenge was to manage time and tiredness (mine and the baby's). My biggest reward was to have been able to breastfeed my three kids for two years each. No other jobs can give you this ability and this relationship with your child.

How did the experience of being a mum change your approach to your business?

I learned that I couldn't do everything! I started to say no to interesting projects, just because I couldn't handle it and the kids at the same time. I was obsessed with my work, and I started to get obsessed with my children's education!

How did you adapt your work style after your second and third pregnancy?

Very easily: I reduced my amount of work. With the third child I had a caesarean and had to take three months off. I nearly died… then work didn't seem so important anymore… After that, I worked for about five hours per day, no more, but intensely! Now that my children are teenagers I am back to normal and I work almost 14 hours a day…
There is time for everything: your children and your work, just be careful to take the time for your children before it's too late. I didn't miss that time like most of my friends. I spent lots of time with them, even if I was working, but I was there, I've always been there, and they knew and know it. This is what makes my work so special: I can decide when my kids need me (and my time) and when they don't.

If there is one thing you would have changed to prepare better for your role as a self-employed mother, what would that be?

I should have known what my rights were. I didn't really pay attention to maternity leave and other benefits one could get. That might have helped me for the first kid: I didn't for example know that a nanny would be paid by the government and that I had the right to get one.

Can you give one important piece of advice for future self-employed mothers?

Don't give up! Your children need you; your clients can always find someone else!

Anna Kamay

- An independent curator, cultural manager and producer, currently based in Armenia, who organises community-based art projects with the goal of using public space and contemporary art to meet local needs.
- Anna curated two major exhibits tackling the issues of Syrian refugees in Armenia and Nagorno Karabakh: "The Newcomers: Syrians in Armenia" (2016) and "Home to Home" (2017). She is the founder of the first international contemporary art festival of Stepanakert, Artsakh Fest, aimed at overcoming the isolation of the conflict-ridden region and revitalising the abandoned State Drama Theatre which once used to be the community centre of the city. Currently she's working on establishing an experimental art residency for mothers in arts called "Juggling Dinosaurs", looking for ways art workers can reconcile their artistic practice with motherhood.
- From Yerevan, Armenia; after seven years of living in Morocco she moved back to Armenia in 2015.

How did your first pregnancy change your work?

I gave birth to my first child in 2013, the day after taking maternity leave, and since I worked full time, I had no time to prepare for the postpartum period: wash the baby clothes, do some "nesting", clean the house, get a stock of supplies for when the baby comes, etc. I did have nausea and vomiting, craving Armenian food while living in Morocco throughout the pregnancy, but that did not affect my work as I was otherwise feeling well. I resumed my work online from home a couple of weeks after the birth and I started going to the office with a flexible schedule and with the option of having my daughter with me (thanks to the baby carrier) a month later. When my second child arrived (unassisted freebirth at home) I was working mostly from home being a freelancer, so I had a full babymoon while my partner took over the responsibilities like housework, caring for my six-year-old daughter, shopping; only answering urgent emails, etc. Now, a month after his birth, I am working part time from home with a flexible schedule.

How did you plan to combine your self-employment with motherhood? Did you prepare for this new challenge before the delivery?

Even though I had friends with children and I read extensively about motherhood, it all came to me as a completely life-altering experience, as I used to travel for work a lot and all of a sudden I was obliged to stay home with a helpless baby with no one to help me. I did save enough money to afford giving birth in a private clinic and stay in a single room with my partner. I really wanted a homebirth, but since it was my first time, I was not sure if I could handle it, and inviting a midwife from Europe would cost me a fortune anyway. My second birth (2020) was a very quick, unassisted freebirth, and I was much better prepared this time.

What has changed in your work style after the delivery? When did you start working again?

I continued working from home a couple of weeks after my first child was born, occasionally going to the office, which was close to our house, but it was a very flexible schedule since I could do most of the work online from home. I never went back to working in an office since then, working as a freelancer for the past seven years in Morocco and Armenia.

Was what you imagined about being a self-employed mum before the delivery different from your reality after the delivery?

I thought I would be able to return to work much sooner both times after birth, but then I realised it was impossible if I wanted to mother my children practicing attachment parenting, i.e. breastfeeding on demand, co-sleeping, not following the "cry it out" method, etc. Luckily, even without a paid maternity leave, which is non-existent for self-employed people, I managed to balance my work and motherhood. The baby carriers helped me tremendously because I was able to carry my babies everywhere and breastfeed them on demand. Having a supportive partner is another aspect I cannot omit. Even though I made it without the help of my daughter's father, with my current partner and the new baby, it's much easier for me to navigate (double) motherhood and work, and I wouldn't even think of having a second child without a partner who'd be sharing the parenting responsibilities with me equally.

What was your biggest challenge and your biggest reward in your first year as a business owning mum?

The biggest challenge was leaving my daughter with a nanny or the grandparents in Morocco, since my parenting style is different, and I was worried about the way my daughter would be treated. The biggest reward was the relief of being able to be mobile and out and about with my child thanks to babywearing.

Do you think it would be easier to combine your work and motherhood if you lived in your home country rather than in Morocco?

My mother died last year, but even when she was alive, leaving my child with her was out of question, since my mother had health issues. My only support both in Armenia and Morocco are my friends, except that now I have a fully supportive partner.

Did you ever feel overwhelmed by stress or exhaustion in your first year as a mother and a business owner? What did you do to deal with it?

It was truly overwhelming most of the days in the first months after the birth. I needed emotional support as well as help with household tasks. I received support from friends, and a housekeeper that I was able to hire in Morocco made my life much easier too.

How did the experience of being a mum change your approach to your work, your customers, or your business partners?

Before becoming a mother, I was quite judgemental of other parents, especially mothers about their parenting methods. Both in Armenia and Morocco it is still common to shout at children and even spank them when they misbehave, etc. I considered my colleagues who would bring their children to work as non-professional. Now I am more empathetic about other parents' choices and I am fully solidary with working mothers knowing that they carry the heavy load of parenting, work, housework (unpaid labour), mostly alone (in conservative countries mostly, but also all around the world), not mentioning the mental load, which is often invisible.

If there is one thing you would have changed to prepare better for your role as a self-employed mother, what would that be?

I would be sure my partner is 100% on the same page with me to support me before deciding.

Can you give one important piece of advice for future self-employed mothers?

Try to negotiate a flexible schedule if possible, to be able to work from home as much as possible, and get a baby carrier—that will make your life so much easier.

Ambika Gupta

- Founder and creative director of The A-Cube Project (www.thea3project.com), an award winning, event-designing company that has been styling spaces and social events since 2012 (it was ranked among the top 10 women designers and planners in India), and House Of A-Cube (a luxury event furniture rental company established in 2019 with furniture and props catering to the needs and demand of the wedding industry).
- Tedx speaker, international speaker at wedding conferences, columnist for a bridal magazine, a masterclass teacher, and a full-time wedding designer.
- From Chennai, India

How did your pregnancy change your work?

I had a planned pregnancy. Being a workaholic, I wanted to take time off and truly enjoy my pregnancy. I had enough savings and my company was young back then. It was just two to three years old. I was a single-woman army at that point, running the show, with people that I would hire on a project basis.

So, I took a break when I got pregnant. I prepared myself that I won't be working for one and a half years including my pregnancy. I, however, kept the marketing and social media handles active and had a lot of pending content that I kept posting. When client calls would come, I would say my calendar is full and would guide them to other people. I kept the credibility alive and kept posting good work in gaps.

Pregnancy obviously changes everything for a bit; your life revolves around an unseen human developing inside of you. I had spotting in my ninth week and had to go on complete bed rest. From working all the time and having a creative brain that was constantly fuelled by amazing projects, to suddenly being in bed all day, was a major lifestyle shift. Having said that, I always knew that I'm going to work all my life, so I most definitely wanted to take a break and enjoy my first pregnancy and experience it fully.

How did you plan to combine your self-employment with motherhood? Did you prepare for this new challenge before the delivery?

No matter how much you plan, I truly believe that nothing can ever fully prepare you for the changes a child will bring, while pregnant or once born. Yes, mine was a planned pregnancy, but nothing could ever prepare me emotionally for it, it can't for anyone, I guess. Financially, it can be overwhelming how a tiny human being can have so many expenses, but we were blessed with enough and that department wasn't an issue largely. I did go for prenatal classes and I did exercise a lot, and I enjoyed my pregnancy as planned. It was more enjoyable when I got the green signal from my doctor post the fifth month to exercise and do whatever I want. I was on bed rest before that (due to spotting) and that was truly depressing in many ways.

I had a normal delivery and I worked hard for it. However, I suffered from postpartum depression once I started weaning around the ninth month. Like I said, you can only prepare yourself with knowledge about symptoms etc., but nothing can prepare you for this new range of emotions you will experience. So, it's always good to go with the flow and to be informed. Being informed is probably the best thing you can do for yourself as a new mother. So, when there is a symptom in any department, you have the awareness to take a step towards it.

What has changed in your work style after the delivery? When did you start working again?

I resumed work when my daughter was seven months old. I was handling my first ever wedding at a five-star property. I took a room at the hotel and had my babysitter with her. I still remember running helter-skelter, pumping milk in the room, sterilising the bottles and all that, so she could be fed, and then running back to the banquet to get work done.

Imagine being in the middle of a setup and realising your breasts are full and you need to pump again before you leak. I don't know how I did it, but I guess the universe blesses mothers and women with the ability to multitask and do the impossible. Once I was able to take the plunge with my first big event after having my daughter, Shanyraa, things got a lot more manageable. I believe it's about taking the first step and getting some help. The fear of the unknown haunts us more than we can imagine. As most entrepreneurs are sticklers for perfection, they can get caught in a catch-22 situation if they over-procrastinate. So, it's best to write down things and pen down possible outcomes or difficulties. Hire professionals in spaces which need help. That could even be a babysitter in this case, and then do your work more professionally!

What was your biggest challenge and your biggest reward in your first year as a freelancing mum?

My biggest challenge was fighting the constant mother's guilt syndrome! I think women are so hard on themselves, even before society adds pressure, we add unrealistic expectations and pressures on our own shoulders to match the image we have built over the years of how a mother should be. I feel no two mothers can ever be the same, and each mother tries to do things to the best of her capacity. It's important to acknowledge and accept how much you can and cannot do. It took me a while to wrap my head around that.

The biggest reward was that my business grew manifold after the birth of my daughter! I got my angel's luck! And the way I moulded my daughter, she was quick to adjust to a working mother. Quality time over quantity became a norm, and I made sure she was close to the rest of the family. So, if I wasn't there, she was still comfortable. The biggest challenge was getting over my own bullshit in my head, and the biggest reward was seeing that eventually everything falls in place. The way you mould your child is how they become. So, talk to them and be honest with them and yourself.

Do you think the legal and social system in your country made it easier for you to combine running your business with being a mum?

Most definitely it is easier to raise a child in my country i.e. India. Having a full-time domestic help is a blessing for a working mother. We don't have any strict laws in our country for mothers and pregnancy. Especially if you are a business owner, you are free to do what you like. It is definitely a boon to have affordable, full-time, domestic help around your baby.

Having said that, in Asian countries and more so in India, the stigma and expectations put on a working mother are manifold. Although it's easier to manage a baby here with domestic help, women do find it very hard emotionally to balance societal expectations, families and work. It can cause an emotional upheaval. Although that is changing drastically, I can say that public mindset is a huge "Con" in my country!

How did being a mother influence your business growth and interactions with your customers?

For me, motherhood has been a rewarding experience in many ways with regards to my business. People take me more seriously now! I think people associate childbirth with magic. And they believe a lot more in me now, when they see me as a successful and knowledgeable mumpreneur! Though they did believe in me initially as well. They do look at me with a lot more confidence now.

Motherhood definitely adds the seriousness and dependability edge to your personality. I feel you also become a lot more empathetic and understand raw human emotion a lot better once you give birth to a child. And that ability to connect with people based on knowledge, perseverance, or even just raw emotion comes even more naturally after childbirth. So, on the client servicing front it has helped me a lot.

On the flip side, most definitely I'm not a single human anymore. Life and timing revolve around the little one. I was a lot more free earlier and I could stay late, or socialise, or didn't have to think about responsibilities before. That aspect definitely changes when you become a mother. That's the reset in your personality you need to be OK with and prepared for.

How did the experience of being a mum change your approach to your business?

Well, for one, I started investing in savings a lot more. I started actively looking into wealth management. However, earlier I would aimlessly store savings or spend them on material things. I also take my business a lot more seriously, so that I can leave a legacy for my child. It has definitely changed my mindset.

If there is one thing you would have changed to prepare better for your role as a self-employed mother, what would that be?

I think one thing I would most definitely like to change is making sure that my partner was equally prepared and excited about bringing in a new life. In my case, even though it was a planned pregnancy, I feel my partner succumbed to the pressure of an Indian household and dominating aunties. But he wasn't really prepared to be a father. Though he dotes on our daughter now, our relationship went through a lot of upheavals because we were young and did not know how to handle a baby who was encroaching on our time as a couple and just to strike a balance between us, work, life, and a child. It was overwhelming and I do wish he was on the same page.

Can you give some important piece of advice for future self-employed mothers?

Set realistic expectations for yourself. Don't compare your child and motherhood with others. Your circumstances are unique and so are you and your child. Your child will always love you and they won't remember things till they are four years old, later in their life. So, it's OK to miss a few things and not beat yourself up about it. Pen down your thoughts when a project at work seems daunting, and take it head-on. Take help wherever you can, don't try to be a martyr! You had a baby; you are already a warrior queen. Embrace your new beginnings, accept the life shift, and make it a new kick-ass life. Co-parent with your partner if your circumstances allow. Keep a periodic check on your health, vitamin, and hormonal levels 'till a year after you stop weaning. Last but not least, there is no manual to be a perfect mother; all you can do is your best, and remember that being a mother doesn't take away the fact that you are a human too, with expectations and desires—so don't be too hard on yourself, and go kick some ass at work!

Mariana Ciocca Alves Passos

- Translator and community interpreter (www.linkedin.com/in/marianapassos) working with the language pair English-Portuguese (Brazilian)
- Translates technical texts in IT, education (e-learning), mobile apps localisation, and interprets in the field of public services in Ireland for Portuguese speakers who don't speak English
- Born in Brazil, currently living in Ireland

How did your pregnancy change your work?

Pregnancy certainly made me more tired, but in general it did not change my work so much. I was also lucky that I did not have any sickness or complications during any of my pregnancies. As a freelancer, I decide my working hours, so even hospital appointments did not impact on my deadlines. My work is a desk-job mostly, so when my bump started to grow bigger, I just had to adjust the way I was sitting and take regular breaks to stretch to avoid pain in my legs and back. Oh, and I had to make sure I slept enough hours because I felt really sleepy.

How did you plan to combine your self-employment with motherhood? Did you prepare for this new challenge before the delivery?

I planned to have a break after delivery as I was sure I would have to adjust to what motherhood entailed, and I was ready to stop completely if necessary. You never know if the baby might need special care or demand too much attention. As I had just moved to a new country, I was still not aware about how social welfare worked, so I did not know if I was entitled to any maternity benefits. So, financially, my husband and I made plans in a way that we would not need my income to live. We could live well on his wage alone. As much as I was trying to prepare myself mentally and emotionally, I don't think I was ready when the baby was born. Motherhood ended up being more demanding than I thought. I only came to terms with the fact that my life and daily schedule were going to be different forever many months after my baby was born.

What has changed in your work style after the delivery? When did you start working again?

Translation is a trade that relies on brainpower. Sleep deprivation took a toll on my brain in a way I wasn't prepared for. I took steps then to help my baby sleep better, organising her routine with naps and feeds during the day, and she slept through the night before she was six months old. That is when I felt like my brain was working well enough for me to go back. Now, there are many methods used to train babies to sleep better. I chose the Baby Whisperer because it sounded gentler than the others I researched. It definitely gave me more peace that I could work some extra hours if necessary because I could trust my baby was not going to wake up every hour at night. In the end, I stopped working for the equivalent of a maternity leave for my first two babies, and that worked well. The third baby was a completely different ballgame.

How did you arrange your day to be able to work and take care of your child?

I decided earlier on that my baby would take priority over my work. So, when I went back to work, I was full time with the baby during the day, and I worked after putting her to bed (and during her naps if my deadline demanded it). My babies always had early bedtimes (8 pm at the latest,) so I had at least four hours a day to work. My availability decreased, of course, but that was also planned. By doing this, I did not struggle with guilt as I know some mothers do when they go back to work, because my primary focus was still my baby and children.

How did being a mother influence your business growth and interactions with your customers?

What drove me into freelancing as a translator was the flexibility. Being a mother certainly slowed down my business growth, but that was something I planned for. I knew I could not embrace the whole world with a child stuck to my breast and another little one (or two) running around my legs. It was a professional decision to accept only what I knew I would be able to handle. I could have taken the route of putting my babies in childcare and work more hours a day, but two things made me decide against that. First, my children were my priority and we did not need my income to live—and I know that is not true for every mom; some really need to work to pay their bills. Second, childcare is expensive where I live (Ireland), so especially after having the second child, I would end up working more hours just to cover childcare costs. I was just honest with my clients saying that I was going to be less available than before, and that did not negatively impact my relationship with them.

What was your biggest challenge and your biggest reward in your first year as a freelancing mum?

Surviving the sleepless nights was hard, but understanding that being a mother has changed me as a person was a great challenge too. And coming to terms that it was OK to prioritise my children over my work too. Nowadays there is a lot of pressure for women to be successful. Motherhood changed the way I see success. I wasn't thinking about making more money, having more visibility, or even having big clients, not even having a perfect life. Success now was about balancing the professional and the mother. Seeing my baby growing and developing was definitely rewarding, but finishing a project for the first time gave me an amazing sense of accomplishment. For the first six months, I was stuck with tasks that seemed endless: laundry, cooking, cleaning, feeding, changing diapers. Those are the type of tasks that as soon as you finish them, you have to start the same thing over and over again. There is no end! Back to work, I felt like I could finally have a finished product, and it was really refreshing.

Do you think combining your self-employment with motherhood would be easier in your home country?

I am not sure. Many things would be different. I would likely have more support from the family in looking after the children, and back in Brazil I could have childcare for free. Maybe if I was there, I would work more hours because I could put the children in childcare earlier. But both countries have maternity benefits for the self-employed, so my time at home after the delivery probably wouldn't have been different. Anyways, I feel like the quality of life is much better where I live now.

Did you ever feel overwhelmed by your responsibilities as a business owner and a mother? If so, how did you deal with it?

As I said, I try not to accept more work than I can handle. That is my way of not being overwhelmed with work. I have certainly felt the pressure as a mother. What solved that was good communication between my husband and I to ensure we both understand that the responsibility for the children is ours, not just mine. It is not just because he works outside the house and I usually work from home that I am the only one who looks after the children (and the house.) Even with babies, the only thing that only the mother can do is breastfeeding, if she decides to do so. All the other tasks involving the house and the baby can be shared, and that should be discussed and clearly agreed between both partners. It helps a lot when we, as mothers, feel that we are not juggling everything alone.

If there is one thing you would have changed to prepare better for your role as a self-employed mother, what would that be?

Knowing what motherhood demands of me, I would have been less harsh on myself. I mean, feeding a newborn baby is almost a full-time job! You spend some good eight hours a day sitting with the baby on your breast—and that is probably the same for those bottle-feeding. I still expected myself to have my meals cooked and the house perfectly cleaned having had only a few hours of broken sleep just because I was at home all day. My thought was always comparing myself to others, "This and that friend have more children than I do, and they manage. I can do it as well." As it turns out, I couldn't, and I struggled with accepting my limitations, and I also struggled with asking for help. I would have definitely enlisted help, paid or not, to make sure at least my house was clean. I only had someone to clean the house when I had my third baby, but I see now that it would have made my life much easier since the first. Even if it was just for the first few months.

Can you give one important piece of advice for future self-employed mothers?

Find out what your priorities are and plan accordingly. If your priority is your baby and your family, plan your schedule, your events, your earnings accordingly. Some women will still be very business-focused after having children and that is OK. For some, that will mean sharing responsibilities of the business with a business partner or sub-contractors while the baby is still very small and there is no chance of a routine. For others, it will mean paying someone to care for the child and the house so you can devote more time and attention to work. Motherhood changes the way we see the world and experience life. But each life circumstance is different, so you have to make decisions that will be good for you, your family, and your business. Good communication is key to not feeling overwhelmed both at home and at work. And talking to other people who are going through the same process helps us see that we're not alone in this struggle. It is a struggle to find that balance, but it is rewarding both in the professional and in the motherhood aspect of life.

Cyville Harriette F. Jaum

- Owner of CJ Virtual Assistance Services (www.cyvillejaum.wordpress.com)
- Offers virtual assistance services such as SEO, social media management and marketing, content creation, administrative tasks
- From Philippines, based there as well

How did your pregnancy change your work?

I stopped working because I had a very sensitive pregnancy. My doctor advised me to take bed rest.

How did you plan to combine your self-employment with motherhood? Did you prepare (mentally, emotionally, financially etc.) for this new challenge before the delivery?

Nope. I was not financially prepared because it was an unexpected pregnancy.

What has changed in your work style after the delivery? When did you start working again?

There are so many changes after the delivery. I had to apply for a job that offers part-time work. I started working six months after my baby was born.

Was what you imagined about being a self-employed mum before the delivery different from your reality after the delivery?

Yes. I thought being self-employed is easy, but it was not. As a mother and a self-employed person, you need to balance your time with your child and time for work.

How did you arrange your day to be able to work and take care of your child?

I always plan ahead. I strictly follow my schedule to avoid backlogs.

What was your biggest challenge and your biggest reward in your first year as a freelancing mum?

The biggest challenge is to have time for my son and work because it was not easy juggling my time as a mother and as a freelancer. The biggest reward is when I was able to earn more money at home compared to working in an office.

Do you think the legal and social system in your country made it easier for you to combine running your business with being a mum?

Nope. The social system in the country has no support system for this kind of job like freelancing.

How did the experience of being a mum change your approach to your business?

I am more patient with my job and I now know how to juggle my time.

If there is one thing you would have changed to prepare better for your role as a self-employed mother, what would that be?

I think I would have enrolled in more training so that I could develop and enhance my skills.

Can you give one important piece of advice for future self-employed mothers?

You always need to be strong and positive. Don't be afraid to try new things and have the willingness to learn more, because when you learn more you gain more knowledge and experience that will make you a successful person.

Daniela Helguera

- Owner of DH Translations (www.dhtranslations.com)
- Certified professional English-Spanish translator, reviewer and subtitler working with technical and marketing materials in the life sciences, more specifically, health, environment and tourism sectors
- From Argentina, based there as well

How did your pregnancy change your work?

When I got pregnant with my first child, I was working—as a telephone interpreter—six hours per day on a fixed schedule for one language provider and freelancing for local translation agencies the rest of the time. I worked until the second trimester of pregnancy, and then, I just stopped working when I felt I needed more time to prepare the baby's stuff; her bedroom and all that. I first stopped working with the interpreting agency because I had signed a contract with them and I had to terminate it formally. I remember my PM back then congratulating me and telling me that she had six kids herself! And I remember I had such an awful fear to not be able to come back then that her words were such a relief for me. I also received lovely messages from my PMs in the local agencies here, and I remember a colleague there telling me to let them know I'd be having a baby and ask them to "wait for me." I got nothing but nice words from them, too. I took six months off, but partly because I wasn't the breadwinner in the house. I relaxed big time. Otherwise, I wouldn't have taken so long.

With my second child, it was different because I knew I would stop working with local agencies after having the baby, purely for monetary reasons. I had started to get in touch with agencies abroad and I decided that—with two kids in the house—I'd be working fewer hours for the same or more money. So, after baby number two, I said goodbye to local agencies. And it was my first smart move, so to speak. So, my pregnancy changed my work for the better because even though I enjoyed working with local agencies, now I had the urge to work less for more. And I did it.

How did you plan to combine your self-employment with motherhood? Did you prepare for this new challenge before the delivery?

To be honest, I didn't prepare much, except for the baby stuff, bedroom, clothes, etc. that we had to buy or get ready anyway. Life felt very intuitive at that time, in the sense that I didn't know how to anticipate myself much because everything was so new, and we were so clueless in almost everything that we only wanted to get organised and have a routine in place. I'm truly a supporter of the belief that routine gives people (especially kids) safety and calm. As I said, I wasn't the only one working at home, but my husband did go back to work a few weeks after our first baby was born. We had decided that I'd wait to recover a bit from the sleep changing patterns to see if I could feed the baby without major problems or frustrations, etc. Eventually, life was kind of back on track again and I emailed the PMs to let them know (as I'd told them I'd do) that I was partially available. And I began to take up work again, and I worked when baby was sleeping or playing in her baby crib. Then when she was eight months and I was accepting more and more work, I hired a babysitter, and that was my other big smart move regarding motherhood and work. I still count on a nanny to get to work.

Do you think your work style has changed again when you gave birth to the second child?

Yes, my work style has changed after the second one. I learned—had no choice, no time, actually—to relax about petty matters, to be less obsessive with double checking absolutely everything and wasting time in things I used to do when I had all the time in the world to prepare one single project. I became more efficient in that.

How did you deal with unexpected situations, for example when your baby was sick and you had to work?

My rule is to have very good and fluid relationships with my PMs and clients, always, so the first thing is to speak to them at the earliest notice of something not going as planned as possible. I try to organise, schedule, and anticipate as much as possible, but this is not always possible in our profession. The 99.99% of the times I had an unexpected situation with my kids, I was the one dealing with it. I might have requested some new deadline, but I don't remember missing a deadline due to personal unexpected situations.

What was your biggest challenge and your biggest reward in your first year as a freelancing mum?

My first biggest challenge was sleep deprivation and a few tight deadlines I remember I met in a very stressful way; my biggest reward is seeing me get through it all, every time. I've always wanted to be close, physically present, to my babies when growing up, and I'm proud of myself for being there.

Now that they're not babies any more, my biggest challenge is to get in the work mind frame every day, physically and mentally speaking. We live in an apartment, and when they are around it's very difficult for me to concentrate. I work in my bedroom, and that's not so ideal for me. I have colleagues who are very happy in co-working spaces or sharing offices, so I'm considering that possibility for what would be my third big smart move now. I'm looking for a change. Thing is, we are also about to move into a house shortly, which has a separate room I could turn into my office... So I'm literally pondering on the options right now, but I sure need to make a new move now.

Do you think the legal and social system in your country made it easier for you to combine running your business with being a mum?

No. There are no maternity benefits in Argentina if you're self-employed. I pay health care and holidays myself. What helped me—and still does—in Argentina is the devaluation of the peso against the dollar, euro, pound. And that's the main reason I only work with agencies abroad now.

How did the experience of being a mum change your approach to your business?

At some point—not sure exactly when—I began to slow down my times; I stopped being obsessive with reviewing the documents time and time again.

If there is one thing you would have changed to prepare better for your role as a self-employed mother, what would that be?

When I had my second baby, things flowed a bit easier and went back to normal sooner than with my first one. So, I guess we didn't do that badly in the first attempt (when we were so intuitively trying to figure out life). I wouldn't change anything actually; I think things eventually settle down. If you're organised and have a clear idea of where you want to go with your business, you'll eventually find the way and means to get going. And I didn't have a clear idea where I was going, go figure! I only wanted to get back to translating! And that was also enough to get me going again. Now after 10 years of experience, I'm going from "just" a professional translator to an entrepreneur and professional translator. But I think that's more related with the business maturity than with motherhood!

Can you give one important piece of advice for future self-employed mothers?

My advice would be to keep calm; don't try to do everything yourself. Time really flies, and after the first weeks or months, everything seems to fall back in place; it eventually does fall in place! Look for help, if friends or relatives cannot babysit your baby, get a nanny, or try to pay a few hours in a baby day care centre, etc. Those few hours alone with my profession every day have saved me from falling into the "only a mum" sort of life. It's very tempting at the beginning, but then being able to have both is absolutely fulfilling!

Christy Racho

- Owner of Lumiera Solutions (www.lumierasolutions.com)
- A systems and process strategist who helps busy mums organise their businesses
- Based in Ontario, Canada (born and raised there as well)

How did you plan to combine running your business with raising your children before you started? Did you prepare for this new challenge?

This question needs a little back story to make sense. I worked for 15 years in a hospital as an Executive Admin and on September 18, 2015 I was in a car accident. What started as "let's give it a few days to recover," slowly evolved into me off recovering for three and a half years and losing my position at the hospital.

It was honestly a blessing in disguise! I was finally able to take a deep breath, something that was getting harder and harder every day that I worked in my old position.

While I was off recovering, I was tasked with looking into options for what I would do next (after my recovery) that would give me flexibility for symptomatic days, allow me to be home more with my family (my husband Andrew and I, and my two boys and two fur babies), and also give me the flexibility to work with people that I choose and who I believe in.

I was a little naive in the beginning. I thought that I would have it all and it would be easy! After a year of burning the candle at both ends and starting to resent my business, I had to really look at how I was managing my time and where I needed to set up better boundaries.

Mentally and emotionally you have to prepare, but you also have to be careful not to get stuck in the prepare stage. Once I finally got the go-ahead to start working (this was almost four years after my accident), I had to stop planning and start doing, which was a real change for my brain. I had to let go of my need to control everything and to have everything be perfect out of the gates!

Financially I was both blessed and spoiled. I was able to recover some money from my car accident which really took some of the pressure off to build my business quick and fast. The downside to this was that I wasn't required to really push myself to become successful. It's only been in the last three to five months that my business has really taken off and it is in part because of the pressure to succeed (my husband lost his job).

How did you arrange your day to be able to work and take care of your children?

My children are a little older at 13 and 10, but they still need Mummy. It has been a challenge for them to be a little more independent but also a gift that they are able to see Mum strive to achieve her goals and that it takes hard work and consistency; a lesson that we have been able to apply to their work ethic especially when it comes to homework and their studies.

I love having the flexibility to work around our family schedule. Both of my boys play sports and have ADHD, which means they have a few more doctor's appointments than the average bear! I love that my schedule allows me to be there for those appointments and not have to beg my boss to let me have a few hours off to do these things with my kids.

It does mean though, that I have to be very intentional with my time and make sure that I am adjusting my schedule to match my work demands. Sometimes I will put an extra hour in, or I might re-adjust my schedule to absorb the away time. I am a huge believer in time blocking my schedule each day and week to make sure that every task I have to complete has a spot to be completed in. I am also getting better at making sure that I have breaks and downtime in my day which actually makes me more productive.

I think the key is to make a plan and use the available tools to keep your business on track and balanced so you can be a mum first and know that you have a plan. I use a client management system that keeps track of my client's invoices, accounts, leads, contracts, and more. This has been a game changer! The other piece of software that I rely heavily on is Click Up. Every task and piece of my brain is in this place so I am not worrying about what I have to do tomorrow when I am choosing to be in my family bucket.

What was your biggest challenge and your biggest reward in the first year of combining your motherhood with running a business?

My family has always been my biggest supporters. My kids constantly tell their teachers and friends that their mum owns a business and that they should check it out!

For me the biggest challenge was where to start and how to manage all of the pieces without having a clue what I was doing. It is very overwhelming when you first start. You need a website, and if you want to be cost effective, you need to know how to manage the website. You need to have contracts, iCloud space, social media, newsletters, blogs, etc. This can be really overwhelming, and then imposter syndrome starts kicking in!

Honestly, the best decision I made early on was to start working with a coach in my field as a mentor to help me figure out what to work on next. Then to start and finish that piece before moving on to the next thing. I spent money on courses trying to figure all of this out, and in the end, it is as simple as start a project and complete the project.

The hardest part about owning a business and being a mum is balance. Trying to give your heart and soul to a business you believe in and being so excited to see it take flight, but then not being able to shut it off to be Mummy the next minute. There is a lot of guilt that happens here. I was able to identify this quickly and started talking to a counsellor to help me navigate it and learn to balance all of the pieces.

If there is one thing you would have changed to prepare better for your role as a self-employed mother, what would that be?

This is tricky... I think I would have to say build your boundaries early and then never compromise on them. Shut your business down every day at 5 (or whatever you decide) and make sure that when you shut it off, you are completely focused on the area that you are in. I had someone explain this to me as buckets. One for your business, spouse, kids, movement, spirituality, self-care, and health. If any of these buckets starts to get empty, then you need to adjust. (I think the bucket thing is probably the most important.)

Can you give one important piece of advice for future self-employed mothers?

The whole point of being in business is to build a life that you love. It is really easy to throw that out the window once you realise that it's hard. Make sure you still make time to be Mummy (which sounds simple, but it isn't), make sure you build balance, and don't let your life revolve around your business. It's a part of you, not what makes you you!

Anastasia Shnyper

- Owner of the Sialia Global Translation Agency (www.sialia.global)
- Freelance translator at www.shnyper.com (IT and Localisation, Chinese, English, Russian)
- Based in Russia (Volzhky)

How did your pregnancy change your work?

It didn't. I worked until the delivery. In the third trimester I started my own business and accompanied it with my regular freelance job. If we talk about motherhood itself, so the work was changed enormously—I can do it mostly after 8 pm, when my children (I have two boys, aged three and a half years and five and a half months) fall asleep; if the work should be done ASAP during the working day, I do it during their noon nap or ask my relatives to help. It's really hard sometimes.

How did you plan to combine your self-employment with motherhood? Did you prepare for this new challenge before the delivery?

With the first pregnancy, everything was unexpected and unfamiliar, so it was rather difficult to prepare for this. I tried to finish my large projects before the delivery (for example my company's website) in order to do only everyday work routine after the delivery. If we talk about daily working process, I try to do my best with time management, my kids wake up at about 10 to 11 o'clock (lucky me), so I started to work from 6 to 7 o'clock and during their noon nap. So, I can spend about five to six hours a day on work and work every day without weekends. For big and urgent projects, I asked my mum, mum-in-law, and husband (he is self-employed too, but he has frequent business trips) to help me.

What has changed in your work style after the delivery? When did you start working again?

Schedule, as I've already said (before motherhood I could work all night and sleep the entire day after, could take very big projects and do them in a couple of days); some of my working habits, of course. After the first delivery, I took another project while being at the maternity clinic two hours after the delivery, and did it in time. After the second one, it was a little bit harder to get used to, because I needed to be at the office sometimes, but now it's OK; I work remotely most of the time.

Did you ever feel overwhelmed by your responsibilities as a mother and a business owner? If so, how did you cope with it?

Most of the time actually, because I also need to devote time to my self-learning, do some household chores, etc. Time management is all you need. I try to change my activity every 30 minutes, for instance, 30 minutes working, 30 minutes playing with children, 30 minutes cleaning the house, 30 minutes relax and rest. Of course, this system gets disturbed by my two dinosaurs, but it's important to consider this programme, to return to it; it helps to create order in all this mess of responsibilities. And I've noticed if I don't adhere to the schedule, I get anxious and tired more quickly. And it's very important to give yourself some rest, to have hobbies. I'm sure that you'll be more effective as a businesswoman and mother if you're happy and satisfied. Being self-employed, I have great leeway because I decide what to do, how to do it, and for how long.

What was your biggest challenge and your biggest reward in your first year as a freelancing mum?

To combine my work and motherhood, certainly. My business is not ruined by my motherhood and it gives money, and at the same time I can spend time with my beloved children, watching them grow, playing with them, breastfeeding them till two years. It's the biggest challenge of my life and the reward (I hope so) will be in the future.

Do you think the legal and social system in your country made it easier for you to combine running your business with being a mum?

I don't have any social welfare as a businesswoman and mother. In Russia, we don't even have a tax relief during this period (only if you don't get profit), but we have free medical service (for pregnant women and children, and free delivery) and some social welfare for parenthood (it's about $100 per month) that is given to everyone who has a baby 'till he or she is one and a half years old; and a one-time payment (about $6,000) for the second delivery that you can spend on a house, pension scheme, future education for the kid, or get it as a monthly salary for the next three years in equal portions each month.

How did the experience of being a mum change your approach to your business?

I think I became softer in a good way; more loyal maybe. It really helps when working with claims, and of course I started to value my time more precisely—now I always estimate if this case is really worth spending time on; if not, I just do not do it. My business conversations and negotiations have become shorter but more effective.

Can you give one important piece of advice for future self-employed mothers?

Don't be afraid, we people can get accustomed to everything in this life. Love your work, your family, and be bold and self-confident.

Rachel Reiter

- Owner of Hopscotch Branding Studio (www.hopscotchbranding.studio)
- Brand stylist, illustrator, and mentor creating one-of-a-kind, impactful brand personalities for online female entrepreneurs who are ready to uplevel and scale their business
- Based in Adelaide, South Australia

How did your pregnancy change your work?

I was already running a freelance graphic design business from home during my first pregnancy. I was extremely fortunate to have supportive and understanding clients, so that afforded me the flexibility to rest and attend appointments around my workflow.

How did you plan to combine your self-employment with motherhood? Did you prepare for this new challenge before the delivery?

Quite honestly, I don't think you can ever fully prepare yourself for the emotional challenges that come with becoming a mother and having a newborn. It is a huge adjustment period in itself, before including the running of a business as well. With regards to my workload, I notified my clients that I would be having a month off to welcome our baby and arranged to complete any work due during this time in advance. I outsourced a few things to do with the running of the household, such as hiring a cleaner. Friends brought meals and home-cooked snacks too, which I really appreciated.

What has changed in your work style after the delivery? When did you start working again?

I started working within two weeks of giving birth. I worked when baby slept, or between feeds. Although some might say that I pushed myself, working is part of my identity, so it helped me through the early transitional stage of learning to be a mother. Very early on, I learned to snatch snippets of time when I could to work. There was no schedule or routine, which I found challenging, but eight years on, this is still how I work!

Was what you imagined about being a self-employed mum before the delivery different from your reality after the delivery?

Yes, of course! There is no amount of reading, conversations, or YouTube videos that can fully prepare you for becoming a mother. The adjustment required to run a business around a new beautiful life required a lot of patience and discovery. I learned that my time was no longer my own, but was governed by always ensuring the baby's needs were met first. I was able to follow a rhythm which revolved around when baby slept and had to learn to let go of my own expectations if the day didn't quite go as I had planned. At the end of the day, it was really about making a conscious decision to be kind to myself.

What was your biggest challenge and your biggest reward in your first year as a freelancing mum?

My biggest reward was in knowing that although it was a bit of a roller coaster, I succeeded in integrating motherhood while maintaining a business that I loved. It helped me to retain my identity and creativity, despite the usual exhaustion and emotional depletion that naturally comes with new motherhood.

Do you think the legal and social system in your country made it easier for you to combine running your business with being a mum?

Yes, absolutely. It's quite easy to start a business from home, which is perfect for combining business and motherhood. Thankfully, I had everything already set up before I had my babies, so it was a fairly seamless transition. Being able to run the business from a home setting allows me to be fully present for my children and have the flexibility to work at times of my own choosing.

How did being a mother influence your business growth and interactions with your customers?

Becoming a mother certainly has made me more patient and empathetic towards others' situations. Generally, my clients are other mothers running their businesses at home, so I am able to connect with them in a meaningful way. I am able to form close relationships with my clients (who often become friends), which makes communication open, honest, and easy.

How did the experience of being a mum change your approach to your business?

Becoming a mother has made me much more time efficient in my business. I'm conscious that every minute spent on my business needs to be meaningful and in some small way be moving me forward in a clear direction. I'm more conscious of who I work with and how I want to have an impact on the world.

If there is one thing you would have changed to prepare better for your role as a self-employed mother, what would that be?

As I mentioned, I honestly don't believe there is anything that can prepare you for becoming a mother, let alone caring for a newborn and running a business. I think talking to others who have gone through a similar experience would have been helpful. That way, you may be able to adapt a strategy someone else has discovered to suit your own situation. At the time, I had very few business connections other than my own clients.

Can you give one important piece of advice for future self-employed mothers?

Remember that your children are only young for such a short time, and you are never more loved than when they are little.

I truly believe that we can have it all, and do it all, but just not all at the same time. Concentrate on small steps that will help you achieve your business dream, but also be mindful that sometimes we need to let go of our own expectations. Small steps are still steps in the right direction.

Magdalena Stojer-Brudnicka

- Conference interpreter and translator (German-Polish)
- Coordinator of international projects for adults and children
- Lives in Warsaw (born in Silesia), Poland
- Works mostly in Germany and Poland

How did your pregnancy change your work?

Pregnancy itself didn't change my work style almost at all. I worked as usual until the last day of my pregnancy. I worked a lot, travelled a lot, both for business and leisure, including by plane, and I led a very active lifestyle. Many people would ask me how it is possible that I'm so active. I would simply answer: "Because I am active." Of course, you need to adjust your activity (also in business life) to your health conditions and to your well-being, but if the mother and baby are healthy there's absolutely no reason to stay at home on a sofa as soon as you reach the third month of your pregnancy.

Unfortunately, pregnancy in Poland is often viewed as an illness. My midwife also tried to convince me to take a sick leave when I was in the sixth month of my pregnancy. In vain. Ten days before the due date (I have a congenital heart disease, so from the very beginning of my pregnancy it was clear that I needed to undergo a C-section), I was interpreting at a large conference in Warsaw. Other interpreters were joking that the German booth is served by three people. Of course, in some cases I had to adjust slightly to my "new" situation. Nearly one month before delivery I had my "last" interpreting job in Germany, and instead of going by train as usual, I travelled by car. It was a faster option, and I didn't have to carry my suitcase when changing trains.

At the beginning of my pregnancy I had many doubts: How long would I be able to work? What will happen if my clients find out that I'm pregnant? Will they stop working with me? Luckily, all these concerns proved to be unfounded and the opposite turned out to be true. Few times when accepting an order, I said: "I think this will be too late and I'll be in advanced pregnancy, so I don't know how I will be able to work." But nearly always the response would be: "Accept it, and if something happens, we'll think about it later and search for another solution." And that's what we did. For the last orders before my delivery, I always had an emergency contact that could substitute for me. I never had to resort to that solution, but the fact that I had someone who could stand in for me and take over my responsibilities gave me a great sense of security, as well as comfort and confidence that I wouldn't let my customers down.

And then, after my baby had arrived, I had to slow down, at least at the beginning. Exactly one month after the delivery, I had my first interpreting job in Berlin that would take several hours. The whole trip by car took nearly the whole day. Many people told me that I'm crazy or even irresponsible, but my husband and my parents were fully on my side, and supported also this decision. To make this one-day trip to Berlin possible my husband took a day off and stayed at home with our baby. My parents joined us in order to help us. My mum stayed with my husband and our baby, while my dad travelled with me as the second driver (on that day I had to drive as far as 1200 km). Before that day I regularly pumped my milk to leave enough food for my baby. Of course, just in case we also purchased some formula. For some time, I was also considering taking my baby with me on that trip. Eventually, I gave up this idea, as such a journey would take two or three days and would be more logistically complicated. It could also be too risky for my one-month old baby, as it was in mid-November. All in all, everything went smoothly. My baby didn't even realise that his mum disappeared, and I was happy that I could work again. Of course, someone could accuse me of prioritising my own needs over my baby's needs... But I wouldn't agree with this, because I didn't put my baby at any risk. He was perfectly taken care of. I had to fight with my unruly lactation (what a relief that you can also pump milk in a car!), but this was the moment when I realised that I can be a mum and stay professionally active; that I can really be a working mum. Plus, a happy mum means a happy child. When my son was seven weeks old, we all went to Germany for four days for my interpreting job. Also this time all my concerns were unfounded. My baby took the journey very well and got used to the new place. My husband was excellent at taking care of the baby when I was at work. And I spent every spare moment with them. My colleague, who was working with me in a booth, also supported me and when necessary he interpreted for a bit longer so that I could feed my child in peace. Moreover, my client also turned out to be very helpful. He made it possible for me to arrive with the whole family, ensured that our room was close to the seminar room, etc. It's very important to have supportive and understanding clients.

Of course, in the first year after delivery I had to reduce my workload. But on the other hand, this was a good time to focus on the most important things and in a way to re-evaluate my work and the orders I accept. My biggest concern related to the postpartum period was that I would go out of business and that my clients would find someone else. That's why I wanted to come back to work as soon as possible to prevent this from happening. And I succeeded. All this wouldn't have been possible without my husband. I could always count on him, as he knew that it's very important that I can come back to work as soon as possible. So, with the support of your partner, with good organisation and self-determination you can achieve a lot to be able to reconcile your work and family life and be a happy working mum.

How did you plan to combine your freelance work with motherhood? Did you prepare for this new challenge before the delivery?

I think it's difficult to prepare for motherhood, especially if you're a freelancer. But it's a good idea to do it consciously. In our case, we had delayed the decision to become parents for quite a long time. First, we wanted to get busy with our careers, travel, see the world, buy a flat, a car, etc. It was also important for me to establish my position in the market and acquire a sufficient number of regular customers and regular events where I could work. These stable foundations definitely make your life easier and finally lead you to the decision that's it's the right time to start a family. Before you decide to have children it's worth discussing with your partner how will you share your responsibilities. For example, who will take maternity/parental leave and for how long or how will you share childcare responsibilities when your leave is over, etc.

Of course, your situation after delivery and the personality of your child may force you to redefine your arrangements, but in my opinion such arrangements will help to avoid many misunderstandings later down the road. In our case, we first decided that we would split the leave half-half, but it soon turned out that it wouldn't be the best idea in financial terms. My husband is a full-time employee and works four days per week for 10 hours a day, which makes it easy to support each other or to take turns when it comes to looking after our baby. That's why I chose to take a one-year maternity leave, while continuing to run my business. It was a very good solution for me, because I could work (mostly from home) and issue invoices. From the very beginning we were doing quite well when it comes to sharing the childcare responsibilities. Whenever I had a one-day interpreting job, even in another city (for example in Łódź, which is about 130 km away from Warsaw), my husband would swap that day for his regular day off during the week, and everything was fine. When my job would take several days before or after the weekend, my husband would take a few days off and travel with me. Of course, I couldn't accept all job orders, only enough to be able to continue working, retain my customers, and earn money.

What has changed in your work style after the delivery?

Obviously, at the very beginning I had to slow down. I allowed myself to take a real maternity leave for one month. In this time, I actually didn't do anything related to my business. Then, exactly one month after my son was born, I travelled for my first one-day interpreting assignment to Germany. Afterwards, I tried to systematically reintroduce my previous activities. Of course, very often these were only baby steps. I could only accept one-day interpreting jobs or interpreting jobs that would take several days, but only if my baby and my husband could accompany me. In case of translation orders, I would accept short texts and take on longer assignments only if I could have a longer deadline. There was no way I could translate 15 pages from one day to another. I think you need to be very careful with such an approach. Once I had a deadline for translation, but annoyingly enough, my baby didn't want to take his nap during the day and was very fussy. Of course, it is possible that it was me who was responsible for such an attitude in my child. I took out my stress on him. So, no wonder that this particular day was terrible for both of us. In such situations you shouldn't try to bite off more than you can chew. On top of that I continued working from home as a coordinator for international projects. When necessary, I handed on the baton to someone else only in the final phase when the actual meeting would take place and I wasn't able to attend it.

Everything started to go back to normal once my baby went to the nursery when he was 10.5 months old. First, he would spend about three hours there per day, and after a few months it increased to 6.5 hours. We always made sure that he didn't spend more time there. As I mentioned, my husband works 10 hours per day, so it's me who takes our son to the nursery at 8.30 am and then picks him up at 3 pm. With time, we also found a good solution, so that I could travel for interpreting jobs that take several days. We found a very nice babysitter to help us. It's an older lady recommended by my friend. She raised two daughters of my friend, so she immediately gained our trust as well. Because of her age and her family situation, she wasn't looking for a full-time babysitting job, neither did we want a babysitter for 10 hours per day.

This is what our schedule looks like when I need to travel for work: my husband takes our son by car to the nursery, and in the afternoon, the babysitter picks him up by bus and takes him home where they play and wait until my husband comes back from work. It works very well for us. Our son likes his new aunt and enjoys travelling by bus.

I think it's also really important to make sure your child gets used to travelling. Our son was born in Silesia (southern Poland), and lives in Warsaw. When he was seven weeks old, he went to Germany for the first time. The biggest challenge then was to take a photo of him for his I.D. When he was two, he already travelled by plane 16 times. Travelling, changing locations, and meeting new people is completely normal for him.

On the other hand, in Warsaw we have no one that would help us with the child. My parents live about 400 km away from Warsaw, my husband's parents about 120 km away. Although my husband's brother lives with his family in an apartment in our neighbourhood, he has two children, so he would need some help as well. But my parents helped us and still keeps helping us a lot in the most difficult situations. Sometimes he would stay at my parents' house, for example for one week. My father has already retired, so he could take care of him during the day. Our son always had a perfect relationship with my parents, so he enjoyed staying with them. He never even asked about his mummy and daddy when he was staying with them.

Coming back to my business, once my son was one and a half years old, I started working with the same intensity as before. Of course, now my work time is shorter because I also have other time-consuming responsibilities related to my child. Or maybe I'm more productive now; who knows. Now I travel for work less often, but this is only a good thing. I used to spend two to three weeks per month on business trips, now I travel only once or twice per month for two to up to six days. So, it's not all that bad. *Do you think the legal and social system in your country made it easier for you to combine running your business with being a mum?*

Well, I think it's not that bad, as long as you take care of yourself as well. Of course, I do have some reservations, for example regarding the amount of maternity allowance for self-employed mothers who are on maternity leave. I don't really buy the argument that I should have paid higher premiums before my pregnancy to have a higher allowance, because all in all the result would have been the same: what I would have paid during one year for social and health insurance, I would have later received as a maternity allowance. However, I think it's a great idea that self-employed mothers in Poland can take maternity leave and maternity allowance and still continue working (and issuing invoices). Then the only premium you need to pay is your health insurance. And that's it. We were also lucky enough that we were granted a place in the state nursery. Of course, I could also complain about the state nurseries in my country, for example the large number of children in one group or poor communication between carers and parents, but all in all I think my son is well taken care of in his nursery.

How did you arrange your day to be able to work and take care of your child?

Because I work mostly from home, it's me who takes our son to the nursery at 8.30 am. If I have a very important meeting or a deadline on a particular day, I ask my husband to drive our son to the nursery. At 3 pm I pick my son up. The next three hours are only for us. At about 6 pm my husband comes back home and we spend the evening together or if necessary, I can still work a bit. I usually work also late in the evening, when our son is sleeping. Such a schedule works very well for us and allows me to work freely and effectively, especially between 9 am and 2.30 pm. Everything gets more complicated when our child is sick and can't go to the nursery. In such situations I discuss with my husband who will look after our son on the particular day (or a time slot) and who has a very important task to do at work. My husband is a full-time employee, so he is eligible to a paid childcare leave. This solution isn't really available for me, but in most cases I can schedule my work more flexibly. Until now I could always come up with a good solution. In the most challenging situations we asked our babysitter for help, so that she could come to our son for a couple of hours, or I drove with my son to my parents, where my dad would look after my child for a couple of hours so that I could work peacefully.

Did you ever take your son with you when you travelled for work?

Yes, of course. Our son was seven weeks old when I took him for my first four-day long interpreting assignment in Germany. My husband accompanied us, too. When our son was nearly one year old, he went with me and my sister to a German-Polish project coordinated by me where my sister held some workshops. When I worked with the group, my sister took care of my child, and when I finished, we switched. This solution worked very well for us. We didn't have any problem either when we organised a one-day trip to Berlin and took 30 children with us, plus my baby. It was fantastic. I was very worried if it would work out. Unnecessarily. For example, when we had to quickly change the metro lines, I would take the baby out of the pram and the other children would carry the pram. I didn't have to ask for help, there were always many volunteers that wanted to carry or push the pram. During our one-hour trip by train, the children who took part in that project were entertaining my baby. So, the whole journey went very smoothly. A few months ago, I took my over two-and-a-half-year-old son to a similar event again. This time it was much more difficult to look after him because it's also a more difficult age. Taking care of him now is more challenging. My "no" doesn't always mean "no" to him, he is very curious, etc. But still, I was able to carry out the project and take care of my child.

How did you handle unexpected situations, for example when your child was sick?

Of course, when your baby is sick it's a challenging situation for every parent. Even if you work full time. If there's nothing very important going on during that particular day, we are in a better situation than an employed parent. When you're self-employed, you don't have to run to the doctor and ask for sick leave for you because of your sick child. You can simply take it easy at work and focus on your child. It gets more complicated if you have a deadline or you have an interpreting job in another city on the day your child is sick. In our case, my husband would stay home with our son or we would call a babysitter. Another solution is to call my parents to ask them to come to us or to travel to them. Of course, because of the huge distance between us and my parents it takes about half a day before we can arrange anything, for example to have my father come to us or to arrange our visit at my parents' house. But all in all, it's better late than never. Until now we could always find a good solution in such situations. We had a really big problem only once. Our son was younger than one year. I was halfway through a five-day interpreting job near Stuttgart, and my husband was on a two-day business trip in Berlin.

During our absence my sister came to Warsaw from Krakow to take care of our child. Everything was perfectly planned. My husband was about to arrive in Warsaw by plane in the evening and take over from my sister who had to come back to Krakow to pick up her children that were supposed to come back home from a summer school. Everything would have gone smoothly if my husband's flight hadn't been cancelled at the last minute. It was announced so late that there was no other possibility for him to come back to Warsaw on the same day, be it by plane, train, or by bus. In this case my husband's brother who lives in the neighbourhood took care of our son, and we also called my husband's father to ask him to come to Warsaw (which would take two hours) if we didn't find any other solution. At the same time, my husband together with other passengers of the cancelled plane managed to rent a car at the airline's cost so that they could travel from Berlin to Warsaw. Finally, instead of coming home at 8 pm, my husband was home at 2 am and took over from the uncle. Today we laugh when we think about this situation, but back then, of course, we were far from laughing. One could think that we were irresponsible by going together at the same time for a business trip. In fact, the opposite is true. We made sure that our son had very good care, we planned for several emergency solutions, and we could act very quickly. Of course, we wouldn't have done it without the help of our family, but on the other hand, if you're a parent and want to continue to work, you do need support of others, be it family, babysitters, or carers. It's good to be aware of it from the very beginning: without a babysitter or a nursery you can't come back to your usual work, even if you work from home.

What was your biggest challenge and the biggest reward in your first year as a freelancing mum?

The biggest challenge for me was the breastfeeding. Unfortunately, my work involves business trips which are more or less often, longer or shorter, but in the end, these are still trips and I wouldn't be able to continue to work without travelling. In the first months of my baby's life I would only travel for several hours. But even such a trip was challenging. A breast pump was my indispensable travel companion. Of course, pumping milk in a toilet (in a hotel where the conference is held or in a petrol station) isn't the most pleasant thing to do, but sometimes you have no choice. I was grateful that such a solution exists and makes my work possible. Regarding special moments, apart from the successful orders that I completed to a certain extent together with my baby (as described above), there were definitely situations when I planned to decline an order, but my customer was insisting that I come and take my baby with me.

If there is one thing you would have changed to prepare better for your role as a self-employed mother, what would that be?

Maybe to live closer to my parents? But it's not possible in our case—so that's not it. Maybe also moving to a flat or house with a garden which would definitely make our life easier in many cases. But this wasn't possible for us—so that's not it either. All in all, I think there's nothing I would have changed. I think that you can't prepare for this role because you can't really understand how your baby will change your life. Maybe I would have started to search for a good nursery in our neighbourhood and for a good babysitter much earlier, just in case.

Can you give one important piece of advice for future self-employed mothers?

Establish your position in the market and don't be afraid of changes that will happen once your baby is born. If your customers are satisfied with your work and want to continue collaborating with you, they will still do so once your baby is born. Check what are you entitled to (maternity benefits, etc.). Find out how other mothers are coping and create your own system based on your preferences, your work style, and your baby's personality. Above all, it's important to remember that if you want to continue to work, you'll have to make compromises—with yourself, your baby, your partner, and your customers. But these compromises are achievable. My friend, also a mother, once said that the only truth about parenthood is that you need to "find a way and survive." I totally agree with her.

PART 2: Reflections

Everything is possible if you believe it is:
How to approach your first year as a self-employed mother

When I started my freelance career, I couldn't imagine how I would ever find the time and energy to be a mother. While I was busy growing my business, my friends and relatives were busy growing their families. Their Facebook timelines were packed with tiny bald humans, while my social media brimmed with posts about bold business moves. Writing blog articles, presenting at international conferences, shooting online courses while still working for my clients and developing my skills—this was my main focus for many years. "There will be a right time for everything." This was my automatic response when any of my employed friends or relatives fired a question about having children at me.

Of course, being a freelance professional wasn't the only reason I kept delaying the decision to grow my family. However, the lack of security that comes with full-time employment definitely played a key role. Many of the women I interviewed for Part 1 of this book adopted a similar approach. Our businesses were our priorities for a long time. First, we tried to create a stable environment, for example, by building a financial buffer, by making sure our businesses could survive without our constant attention or by improving our quality of life. Although it's not possible to prepare for motherhood, there's always something you can do in a different or better way. Obviously, buying a car or saving for your maternity leave won't guarantee a smooth journey into parenthood. It can, however, increase your sense of security and boost your self-confidence. And that's often what helps convince you to take a plunge into the unknown.

You can't always plan your family life to the same extent as you can plan your business life. But even when you have to unexpectedly welcome a human being into your territory, you can still take steps to create a safe and warm environment. An environment in which you'll still be able to grow and prosper, but probably on different terms than before.

The chapters that follow will help you learn to walk through this new territory. Based on the stories of other self-employed mothers and my experience, I made an attempt to compile a sort of a guidebook. This is by no means an ultimate set of rules or the only way to successfully combine your business with motherhood. It's simply a bundle of ideas and suggestions that may be useful, especially in you first year of being a freelance mum.

The first days, weeks, or months in your new reality as a mother are usually perceived as the most challenging. After one year of juggling parenthood with your career, you will definitely have figured out what works best for you, your family, and your child. You will become an expert in multitasking, micromanaging, constant business growth, and loving childcare.

Before the Revolution

Getting ready for the unexpected

You can't truly prepare for motherhood or envisage your life as a business-owning mum. However, you can equip yourself with useful tools, ideas, emergency plans, and potential quick fixes that will sit in your arsenal, ready to be deployed at any time. Yet, even this might not be enough to deal with every single event, situation, or feeling that will occur in your new life. Chances are you'll turn to improvising and adapting on the go to be able to survive and grow. And there's nothing wrong with that. The unexpected emotions, circumstances, difficulties, or moments of joy will become an inseparable part of your life as a first-time mother. If you add your business to this new reality, you'll probably end up with an explosive mixture. Luckily, with a healthy dose of caution and the right level of protection, this mixture will eventually become more manageable.

The unexpected schedule

It can be tough to combine motherhood with self-employment if you don't have patience, flexibility, and endurance. However, the key element to success is good health. You'll need to be fit and healthy to take care of your child and your business.

But a good physical condition won't be enough without the right mindset. Whether you believe in the power of positive thinking or not, now is the time to redefine your approach to your business and your responsibilities as a new parent. If the idea of working on your projects at night or typing e-mails to your customers while breastfeeding sounds overwhelming, don't worry. Soon you'll get used to maximising small pockets of time and learn to be fast and efficient. In fact, many mothers work more productively once their time shrinks to the size of their baby's nap. Numerous scientific studies have proven that the secret to productive and efficient work lies in working fewer hours. Now, as a freelance mum, your "fewer hours" might mean three or four hours per day, which might not be enough if you compare it with your earlier work schedule. But here is the bright side: With less time on your hands, you'll learn to prioritise or give up unprofitable projects and activities.

For example, in order to complete my work during my baby's naps and short stretches of time when my husband was at home, I gave up networking and intensive social media marketing for nearly one year. I also resigned from co-organising workshops for translators, as I didn't perceive it as sufficiently profitable to continue. All in all, even though I reduced my work time from eight to about four or five hours a day, I could still secure the same income. Financially I was on the same page, but I failed tremendously in terms of nurturing and building relations. When my daughter turned six months, I decided to hire a babysitter for 15 hours per week so that I could work in more regular time slots. Yet, I still prioritised my health over my business: three days per week I would start my day in a yoga studio practising ashtanga, and only then I would drive back to my home office to focus on work. Surprisingly, I could always meet my deadlines, although I never worked more than six hours per day. A turbo efficiency mode kicked in every time I knew I only have a few hours to complete my tasks before my baby would wake up or before the babysitter would leave.

Reducing your work hours or fitting your work around your baby's routine might be your only option, at least during the first few months. But this doesn't have to be a scary scenario. Working in this way can increase your focus and help you cut down on unproductive activities. Even if now you can't imagine that you could ever get used to working in blocks of 45 minutes or very late at night and early in the morning, you'll quickly adapt to these and many other trade-offs.

Your work schedule might be more stable if you decide to enrol your baby in day care from an early age or if you have a family member that could regularly look after your child. Another solution is to take your baby to your office or watch him or her while working from home. However, this method won't be ideal for everyone. Some babies need constant attention, and some projects will need your full engagement, so multitasking isn't always the best choice. It never really worked well for me, but it turned out to be perfect for several mothers interviewed in the first part of this book. The best approach is to test different scenarios to adjust your work style to the personality of your baby and to the nature of your work. Maybe you'll be able to keep your baby in a carrier or in your arms—like Kateryna and Anna did—while you continue working on your projects, or maybe you'll have to draw a strict line between business and parenthood. There's really no one effective way of arranging your schedule. And you probably won't be able to determine the best way for your situation before your baby arrives.

The unexpected twists and turns

Unpredictable working hours won't be the only building block of your new reality. The health and behaviour of your baby will have the biggest influence on your work performance and habits. You probably hope or assume that your baby will arrive in good health and you won't have any complications during and after the delivery. While it's important to stay positive, drawing up an emergency plan may come in handy too. It doesn't have to be very detailed and only needs to consist of minimal research on the available support options in case you can't go back to work as quickly as you'd like to.

Is there someone who could take over your tasks and your customers if you have to take a longer break? Are you eligible for a decent maternity leave? Will you have any other financial support if you're forced to put your business on hold? Your health and your baby's health are the priorities, so take a moment to draft a Plan B in case you'll need more time to regain your strength and energy.

Even if everything goes smoothly and you're ready to pick up your work where you left off before giving birth, there's still a lot of room for unpredictability. The routine of your baby might change; your child might get sick or become very fussy or very clingy and unwilling to let you do anything without holding him or her in your arms.

One thing you can be sure of is that your baby's behaviour will constantly change. The moment you detect your baby's rhythm and get used to regular downtimes, something unexpected is bound to happen. For example, three naps will merge into one or a long three-hour nap will split into three snoozes. Anything can change any time, so if you're planning to fit your work into your baby's sleep time, consider these ideas:

1. Try not to take rush jobs while counting on your baby's regular nap time. What if your baby decides to change her routine or suddenly cuts down her nap time from two hours to one? This has happened to many self-employed mothers, including me: the moment you rely on regular time off, your day suddenly flips upside down. This could be because of a cough, teething, a growth spurt, sleep regression, or

overstimulation. Be ready to take unexpected courses of action and don't fill your schedule to the brim.

2. Organise a backup network. Have a list of backup partners that would be willing to help you complete your projects in case of emergency. Your backup network can consist of other freelance professionals in the same industry, for example other trustworthy translators, yoga teachers, or designers that you respect and can rely on. In return, you can jump in and take over their projects if they are sick or have to give their full attention to their children.

3. Have a network of friends or family members ready to help you out if you need to quickly finish a job. This could be another freelancer or a self-employed mum, your parents, or your neighbours. Make sure your list of potential helpers is quite extensive and that they live nearby. You never know who will be available on short notice. It's probably much easier if your network includes people who already know your baby and have spent some time with her. Leaving a baby with a complete stranger—even if it's your best friend or aunt—when you need to rush to work could make matters worse.

The unexpected emotions

There's no doubt that giving birth and becoming a mother is a life-altering experience. For many women, it's the biggest transition they'll ever go through. With so many hormonal, physical, and energetic changes going on, it might be difficult to focus on any aspect of your life from before the revolution. Just like your pregnancy, the first few weeks of motherhood will most likely also be marked by swells of unpredictable, contradictory, and overwhelming emotions. Once you get used to your new reality and your hormone levels regulate, these feelings will become less intense. Still, every day spent with your child can send you on a roller coaster of emotions—from joy and pride in one moment to anger, exhaustion, and resignation in the next. This will not only have an impact on your interactions with your child, but also on the way you behave towards others, including your customers or business partners. To get ready for this part of the journey and make sure you can return to your business in as peaceful a manner as possible, you'll need to establish some coping techniques.

One such technique is self-soothing. The main focus here is to involve your senses to calm down. Through touch, taste, smell, sight, and sound, you can generate positive emotions that will balance or reduce your negative feelings. For example, you can try to soak in a warm bath, expose your skin to the sun, or stretch your muscles with yoga poses or simple exercises. Refreshing fragrances can also help in managing extreme levels of emotions. You can equip yourself with essential oils for aromatherapy or products that release your favourite smell. Sometimes, the quickest remedy for any burst of anger or sudden increase in stress levels is to change your perspective. Simply leave the room and go for a quick walk; take your mind and eyes off the source of your intense emotions. Take a deep breath, close your eyes, and try to figure out what is actually causing the negative reaction. Is it your baby who rejects food and doesn't want to sleep? Or is it your expectations about how your baby should act? Is it your stubbornness or the rebellious nature of your child? Is it a lack of help or too much unsolicited advice from friends and family? Is there anything you can do about that?

To find your inner voice and answers to all burning questions, you can try mindfulness or visualisation. Not all methods will work for you in any given moment, so observe your breath, body, and thoughts next time a strong emotion takes control of you. Try several different techniques to figure out what your quickest and most efficient remedy is. Finding your particular cure for waves of emotions before giving birth might help you deal with unexpected emotions and moments once you become a mother.

Although it's easy to understand the cure in theory, the next step is to remember to actually use your preferred coping strategy when you're beside yourself with anger or frustration.

If, for example, you get angry at your rebellious baby who refuses to sleep at her regular time, crushing your dream for a peaceful hour of work, try to disconnect and redirect your energy. Your baby will sleep at some point. Sooner or later you'll get back to drafting your projects, and in few hours your anger and helplessness will be only a distant memory.

In order to continue running your business shortly after giving birth, you'll need to learn to disconnect from negative emotions during your "baby and me time." This way, you'll be able to free your mind, slow your pace, and focus on your work when you finally have the time for it. Otherwise, taking care of your child and serving your customers might get even more complicated and stressful, as accumulated negative emotions will limit your creativity, destroy your motivation, and sap all your energy to work and function in an effective way.

The unexpected strength

No matter what kind of unexpected situations you'll be faced with, remember: All mothers have superpowers! If you think you're not a good multitasker or can't imagine entertaining someone while brushing your teeth or sorting laundry—don't worry. Soon you'll probably find yourself performing this and many other balancing acts. Waking up every two hours at night to nurse your baby only to get up before the sun to work for three hours and then spend the rest of the day with your child? No problem at all. Carrying your baby in a sling while cooking or replying to your customer's e-mails? Also possible. Coming up with a quick and effective solution when you have to leave the house but your baby keeps holding you up and does not want to stay with your partner? Soon, you'll master all these superpowers too.

In fact, there are studies that prove that high levels of oxytocin—a hormone released during pregnancy and postpartum—lead to changes in a mother's brain. That's what makes a mother more aware of all the signals that her baby sends, motivates her to take care of her newborn, and gives her more strength to cope with her new reality. Plus, the more parents bond with their babies, the more oxytocin is released, which further increases their ability to prioritise their child and generate more survival skills. So, your superpowers will come to you naturally, and the more attention you give to your child, the more perseverance and resourcefulness you will have.

In addition to the ability to quickly find effective solutions to problems, you'll also gain many other handy skills, even if you don't have them now. Hormones, instinct, and the necessity to adapt to your new life will reward you with the patience and energy to get through every day and night. Of course, there will be days when you wish someone else could breastfeed your baby, and there will be nights when you wish you could simply sleep without any interruptions. But somehow, anything that appears challenging now—before the delivery—will probably become a piece of cake or a standard part of your routine shortly after giving birth. Even if it seems that you have more than enough on your plate with all the tasks and responsibilities around your baby, your house, and yourself, you can still find the strength to work and run your business. I'll get down to the nitty-gritty of this in Chapter 2, but for now, just rest assured that as long as you and your baby are in good health, you can set up some sort of a system that will help you give enough attention to your child and to your work.

Sometimes your superpowers will fade temporarily. That's why it's worth reflecting on what it is that usually makes you happy and motivated. Is it a good cup of coffee? Your favourite chocolate? Your favourite song? A long chat with your friend? A good night's sleep? Or maybe a few minutes of yoga and meditation? Find your own reliable source of energy and motivation, and be ready to release it when you feel overwhelmed.

Whatever happens, know that you'll have the energy to overcome any unexpected challenges. New skills and new tricks of the trade will pop up without you even realising it. Your intuition will lead you in the right direction, and you'll find your little pleasures and unfailing sources of energy. Simply equip yourself with perseverance and keep going.

The burden of the first year

In addition to constant changes and unexpected turns, the postpartum months are also marked with breathtaking flashes of joy and misery. Maybe your friends have already told you that only the first few months are tough. Maybe you've read that there are several challenging periods in a child's life. Maybe you've heard that the older the children are, the more difficult it gets. Whatever the case, the first year is usually perceived as the most overwhelming. That's the time when you need to adapt to all the changes in your life, both positive and negative.

If, on top of this, you're planning to run your business at the same time, you'll need an extra dose of patience and energy. Don't delude yourself—it's not easy to take care of a newborn, yourself, and your customers, regardless of how much help your family offers. Even if your baby is a silent and easy-going wonder of nature, at some point you'll feel that you're losing it. But after a while, when you look back at those first months, you'll be proud of yourself. You might find yourself reflecting on this period and asking questions such as: Why didn't I spend more quality time with my baby? Why was I so stressed about taking care of her? Why did I try to come back to my old life so quickly? Why didn't I read/study/develop myself/work more? Why didn't I ask for help? Why didn't I sleep and rest more while others were taking care of my baby? Why didn't I insist that my partner takes on more responsibilities at home so I could rest or work?

These or similar (often contradictory) reflections may come to mind once you feel more confident in your role as a self-employed mother. However, before this happens, you'll have to go through many exhausting days. Your body and mind will be faced with endless challenges, and sometimes your reality will be far from perfect. Suddenly, the housework will double or triple and your needs will get pushed to the background as you learn to cope with your new lifestyle and do your best to fit into your role as a mother. It won't be all roses, cuddles, and smiles. The tough moments will surely come, but that's just an integral part of this journey. Tears, doubts, and exhaustion may become your daily companions, but—again—this is totally normal, even if you don't have a business to run. And when you do feel overwhelmed, you have the power to decide if you want to keep immersing yourself in the black hole or get up, dust yourself off, and try to be positive, patient, and calm again.

The first year will only be as tough as you allow it to be. With the right mindset, any burden will quickly turn into a temporary challenge that can be fixed. By now, you already know that mothers have superpowers, so you'll also find your strength to carry on, no matter what happens.

I always thought that the stories about the first year being so tough were just myths. My baby was quite easy-going, my partner was quite helpful, and everything seemed to be running pretty smoothly. In reality, my energy was drained and I barely had any time for anything, but I didn't feel like I was going through a tough period. I probably didn't realise what I was experiencing due to the hormones and my "can-do" approach blinding me. Then, somewhere at the beginning of 2020, when my daughter turned 14 months, I felt like I had just woken up from a long dream. Where had the year gone? Why was I so stressed when my baby didn't want to sleep? Why was I complaining that I didn't have time for my professional development? Why didn't I work harder on my business? Why didn't I read more books, watch more movies? Why did I neglect my husband and relationships with my friends? Where was my mind?

Maybe it was the magic of the glittering new year, maybe taking care of my child suddenly became easier, or maybe it was simply a result of good stress and time management in combination with different hormone levels. Whatever triggered the change, it took me some time to admit that the first year had been both tough and rewarding; stagnant and swift. Even though my business didn't flourish, other good things happened in my life. Even though I couldn't teach my daughter to sleep in her own bed or fall asleep without breastfeeding, I was happy that I found a way to fit my projects in during her nap times. I tried so hard to follow tips and instructions from books about baby care that I totally forgot that every baby is different and I shouldn't expect my daughter to do what is considered "normal". I stressed too much about her development and her sleep pattern, or lack of it. Instead, I could have tried to find a way to adapt to her habits or waited until she naturally became less dependent on me. I kept regretting that I couldn't work eight hours per day anymore, but actually I should have been thankful that I could work only four or five hours and still generate nearly the same income as before my pregnancy. But I didn't see that. And when I woke up from my 14-months-long lethargy, I started writing this book.

Yes, the first year might be extremely exhausting and you'll probably feel overwhelmed by your responsibilities. But you've got this. You'll get through the ups and downs of your journey as a mum and business owner. You'll even enjoy it. The truth is, you can make it through even the most challenging times. But to do this, you'll need to change your mindset and stop comparing yourself, your baby, and your business to others. If you need to cut down on your working hours to be able to spend more time with your baby, you probably won't be able to achieve as much as your friends who work on their businesses full time. Conversely, if you decide to have your baby or toddler play at your side while you work on your laptop, try not to beat yourself up that you can't spend more quality time together. Trade-offs are inevitable, and you'll need to learn to accept them.

Looking back at your old life and wishing you had the same amount of time or the same work pattern as you did before giving birth won't be very productive. Such an approach won't help you move forward. Your daily life will change drastically, but that doesn't mean it will get worse. With good time management, a relaxed attitude, and the ability to listen to your intuition, you can make the first and all the next years truly enjoyable, even if it requires reducing your work time or involving more family members to help with your baby.

Finally, don't focus on what you can't do—because of your baby or freelance work—but rather on what you can achieve regardless of your new responsibilities. Don't fixate on what you're missing or can't carry on, but try to think about all the little things that you're able to accomplish. Gratitude will be your key to survival. Begin to practice this approach before giving birth already, and your transition into a life of a self-employed mum will play out much more smoothly.

The battle of priorities

You are more important than your business. This might sound like a cliché, but ultimately everything boils down to your own well-being. A business can't be sound if the business owner and the main service provider is exhausted, overwhelmed, consumed by stress, or suffering from sleep deprivation. Your business and your customers need YOU at your best, so try to attend to your basic needs first before moving on to help others. This applies not only to your pregnancy and the postpartum period, but to any other phase of your business activity.

The same is true when it comes to taking care of your baby. A stressed and exhausted mother is more likely to have a frustrated and fussy baby. Your mood will influence the behaviour of your child, so try to take care of yourself to be able to give your baby as much energy, love, and attention as possible.

It's easier said than done—I'm aware of that! It took me a while to realise that by neglecting myself I was also neglecting my baby and my business. I didn't have to work immediately after giving birth, but for some reason I was sitting (actually lying on my bed, still in delivery pain) in front of my laptop merely two days after the delivery. It would have been better for all of us (my daughter, my husband, myself, and my customers) if I had taken a long break to recover and fully embrace being a new mother. Instead, I ended up being stressed from lack of sleep and time to finish my projects, which of course reflected badly on my husband, my baby, and the quality of my work. I wish I knew back then that sometimes, you simply can't have it all at the same time. Sometimes it's worth fighting your old habits to open up to new possibilities.

If, like me, you happen to be a workaholic or tend to be overambitious, there are some strategies that you can use to help you learn how to take it easy without taking your job too lightly.

Method 1

Before giving birth, think about how you want to spend the first week with your child. What is the atmosphere at home? What are you doing? Who is with you? How do you feel? Don't think about what you have to do, but what you really want to do. Visualise as many details as possible. What do you think will be the most important for you in the first few weeks? What will be REALLY important?

Of course, you can't predict everything. There might be unexpected complications (difficult delivery, long stay at the hospital) or other issues (problems with breastfeeding, extremely colicky baby) that could destroy your perfect postpartum image. However, try to focus on the bright side and picture yourself with your baby in a safe and healthy environment surrounded by caring and loving people.

Now, is there still place for your work in this vision? What will happen if you put your work on hold for several days? What about several weeks? Maybe months?

What can you do now, before your pregnancy or delivery, to achieve this ideal scenario? Is there any way you can prepare to bring your vision to life? Is there anything that prevents you from making this ideal come true?

For example, you might need to start building your financial cushion a few months before pregnancy or delivery to be able to take a longer break. Perhaps you need to learn to delegate some of your tasks. You could hire and train an assistant—like Maha from Part 1 did—or you could refer some of your customers to your trustworthy colleagues for the period of your absence. This worked well for me. Maybe you could work on only a few projects and rely on your partner's income for some time, which is what several of the women I interviewed did.

Of course, you don't have to put your business on hold during your maternity leave. You can still enjoy your time off while ensuring your business is operating and generating revenue.

To make this possible you can for example:

1. Train an assistant (maybe also a freelancer) to take over some of your tasks while you're on a leave;
2. Hire a sitter for your business (such as BizBabysitter) who will help to manage your activities while you're away;
3. Schedule certain tasks in advance. Depending on the nature of your work, you can schedule some activities before your leave, for example, if you manage social media, you can schedule posts for your clients a few weeks ahead of time. If you're a writer or a blogger, you can write several articles in advance and set up the publishing date;
4. Do a limited amount of work during your leave. You might still be able to take on some tasks if you don't want to fully lose control over your business. As your working hours are probably flexible, you can fit in a number of non-urgent projects or administration tasks while your baby is asleep or when your partner or other family members can look after your baby.

Once you identify which aspects of your life or your personality prevent you from achieving your perfect postpartum situation, you'll be able to reduce their impact and make your ideal scenario more achievable. Sometimes all you need is a few little steps rather than a dramatic, sudden change.

Method 2

If you don't know how you want to approach your postpartum recovery and wish to go back to work as quickly as possible, this little exercise might help you shift your focus:

If you're like most self-employed and ambitious women, you've probably been working hard for a long time to make your business flourish. That's why taking a break or slowing down due to maternity leave or pregnancy might seem like an unnerving idea. But what if this is your gift and the only chance to actually reduce your pace and unwind? Why not look at the months ahead as an opportunity to learn something new about yourself and the world around you? Rearranging your business in a way that gives you more time and fewer worries in the first weeks after giving birth can help you focus on what really matters—you, your baby, and your family. After all, what's the purpose of all the hustle and hard work if you don't have the freedom and energy to spend meaningful time with your loved ones?

No matter what happens and how you decide to arrange your postpartum life, remember your values. What's the most precious to you? What are you working for? What's your goal? Write it down and never let it slip your mind.

Finally, analyse what the worst-case scenario would be if you were to work less or take a longer break. Will your customers really forget about you? Will your business go bankrupt? Are you afraid that you'll feel unproductive and useless? Tap into your anxieties and break them down. Think of ways in which you can eliminate your fear, if fear is the main reason driving your work habits. For example, if you're anxious about losing your customers if you take a few months off, contact them beforehand and refer them to a trusted colleague or your trained assistant to ensure that they'll continue to receive high-quality products or services. Explain why you won't be able to work or why you need to cut down on your work time and indicate when you plan to be at their disposal again. In most cases, if your customers value your work, they'll wait for you and show their enthusiasm once you're back from your maternity leave. That's a huge self-confidence booster!

This is exactly what happened to me. I didn't want to stop working because I was afraid of losing my customers. Instead of taking a real maternity leave, I came up with the rule of three: I continued working only with three customers in the first three months and accepted projects that wouldn't take more than three hours of my time per day. I informed my remaining customers that I was going on a maternity leave and referred them to a trusted colleague. Luckily, they understood my situation and 90% of them continued doing business with me when I returned after three months of absence. Of course, I could choose to focus on the 10% that stopped working with me and consider my decision unwise. But I'm grateful to have found out that most of my customers value my work. They could have ignored my suggestion of working with my colleague and found someone else (cheaper? better?). They could have perceived me as an unstable business partner and decided never to work with me again. Instead, they remained loyal, and my fear of losing my source of income turned out to be unfounded.

Take some time to recognise what the factors are that make you hold on to your work habits. If you feel you'd like to take a break but are worried about your business, build a strong plan of action by delegating your tasks, rearranging your schedule, limiting your work time, hiring assistants, or collaborating with trusted partners. Also make sure that you take steps to reduce your anxiety!

Of course, if you consider your business to be your top priority even after having a baby, all these suggestions might be useless to you. In this case, the right approach for you might be to continue working the same or slightly reduced hours. You'll probably need to rely on a good day care early on or have supportive family members that will look after your baby while you work. Some mothers choose to work with their babies at their side, however, this solution won't work for all babies and all work activities that you're planning to carry out. Try to figure out what will be the best solution for you to be able to return to work as soon as you think you can. If you're planning to leave your baby at a day care, you'll probably have to arrange it well in advance, as in many countries the best options have long waiting lists.

The financial meanders

The main reason many self-employed women find it difficult to focus fully on their journey into motherhood is usually related to their financial situation. With no employer to cover your leave, limited state support, and no guarantee that there will be anything to come back to if you take a longer break, many freelancers tend to abandon the idea of maternity leave altogether. If you've read the stories of the self-employed women in Part 1 of this book, you may have noticed that most of these mothers resumed their work almost immediately after giving birth. Only a few took the time and effort to prepare their businesses for a longer absence in order to retain customers, secure a decent income, and enjoy some time off with their infants.

From a financial perspective, maternity leave is not impossible for freelancers. It simply requires thorough planning, researching, and scheduling. Ideally, you should already start your arrangements a few months before getting pregnant so you can save more if the maternity benefits of your country are not sufficient (or are non-existent) for self-employed mothers.

As a freelancer, maybe you've already built your safety net to prepare for the worst-case scenario. One option is to apply for disability insurance, which will cover you in the event that you become disabled through illness or injury, including any complications after giving birth. In some countries you won't be eligible for disability or short-term disability insurance if you're already pregnant, so research your options thoroughly and plan well in advance. You could also add supplemental maternity insurance to your health insurance to make sure that you continue receiving some part of your income if you're unable to work due to medical reasons. Another option is to follow the advice of many financial experts who recommend that self-employed professionals should always have a buffer worth three to six months of their expenses. This financial cushion can help you through unexpected events such as a sudden loss of clients, late payments, or health problems. You could also use these savings if your maternity allowance is too low or if you need to extend your leave.

The law in each country varies, and depending on your location, you might be eligible for a maternity allowance from the government. For example, in the UK, if you meet the appropriate criteria, you qualify for about 140 GBP per week, and in the Netherlands, you might be able to receive an equivalent of minimum wage for a minimum term of 16 weeks (about 1500 Euro per month). Make sure you know the relevant laws and criteria in your country, and calculate your monthly expenses to find out if you need to take any further steps. In some cases, the benefits you receive from the government will be much lower than your usual earnings, so having a financial cushion or passive income (online courses, books, properties, or other types of investments) will be of great help. If the social system in your region doesn't support self-employed mothers at all, you'll need to set more money aside to be able to take a longer break.

How can you figure out what amount you'll need to save to be able to step away for a few months? Here is a simple formula you can use:

1. Calculate your monthly expenses, both in business and private life.
2. Add about 10% for unexpected payments.
3. Now, multiply this amount by the number of months you'd like to take maternity leave.

This is the amount you'll need to save if you won't be receiving any income during your maternity leave. Now, think how much you need to save per month to prepare for this scenario. For example, if your monthly expenses amount to 2000 Euro and you're planning to take four months off, you'll need to put 8800 Euro aside (that's with the 10% extra from step 2). Let's assume you are able to contribute 600 Euro per month to build that safety net, which means that you'll need to start saving about 14 months before your planned leave. If you do qualify for a maternity allowance from your government, you can deduct that sum from the final result and reduce your monthly savings or the number of months in which you'll be putting your money aside.

You don't have to abandon the idea of taking a break if you're concerned about your finances. With a thorough plan and the right arrangements in place, you can keep your business afloat, enjoy some time off, and retain your customers.

Slowing down won't slow you down

If the financial aspect is not what scares you the most about your upcoming life as a new mother, the next scary thing might be the need to adapt to a different routine. A slower routine on the one hand—in terms of business activities—and a faster routine on the other—in terms of domestic chores and family responsibilities. Yet, slowing down or limiting your work doesn't have to be a bad decision.

Slowing down to refocus and readjust

If your schedule was always packed with activities and your desk full of endless to-do lists for business and private life, the idea of taking a long break might be overwhelming to you. As our modern society worships the concept of constant busyness, it's difficult to step back or consciously choose to travel in a slower lane. Many people perceive hustling and overachieving as indispensable values and allow themselves some time off only after hard work. With such an attitude, you might end up feeling guilty when you take a midday nap or decide to spend a full day to simply be rather than do. However, there are moments in your life when escaping the race and changing into the slowest gear is the most reasonable decision you can make. Pregnancy and the postpartum period definitely belong to that category.

Are you ready to take it slow? Or more importantly, are you willing to refocus and readjust your life and your business? This is usually one of the major challenges for self-employed mothers. Before giving birth, my approach was to simply adjust on the go, but I failed miserably. I suffered and struggled but eventually learned from my mistakes and came up with a new plan. I thought it would be enough to work when my baby was asleep, at least in the first three months.

Officially, I was on maternity leave, but because I couldn't stop being busy, I ended up working with three regular customers. When three months had passed and my maternity leave was over, I continued to work through my baby's nap times for another three months, disappointed that couldn't fit everything into the tiny time pockets. There was simply not enough "baby sleep time" in a day to be able to do yoga, translate, work on my marketing strategy, do some networking and administration tasks, plus top it off with an episode of a favourite series. Deep inside I wasn't ready to slow down and rearrange my life, even though I knew I should.

If you'd rather have a smoother journey into your motherhood and want to avoid feeling frustrated, exhausted, or overwhelmed by your inability to focus on your work and business, below are some strategies you can follow:

1. **Learn to prioritise**

    No matter how much or how little time you're planning to take off after giving birth, you'll need to get ready to change your daily habits. From your work style to social life and time spent on entertainment—many things will have to transform to make space for your new life. That's why you'll need to establish what is most important for you and what can be slightly postponed or removed from your agenda. Once you set your priorities straight, you can eliminate or delegate tasks that don't require your immediate attention or are at the bottom of the priority scale. (You'll find more tips on time management in Chapter 2.)

2. Savour your "business only" time

If you want to complete as many tasks as possible in a shorter time frame, you need to learn to truly work when it's time to work. If you can work only when your partner looks after your baby or when your baby is asleep, you'll quickly learn to make the best use of every minute. Eliminating time killers and unimportant activities will help you focus on your core business and increase your productivity. No matter what's going on around you, try to remember that this is your precious moment to work. Leave online shopping, browsing through pictures of your baby, searching for parenting advice, and scrolling through social media for another occasion. Having only a few hours per day to run your business will teach you to act responsibly and help you reduce or totally eliminate unproductive habits. This is, at least, what happened to me and many other self-employed mothers.

3. Enjoy it while it lasts

You'll have only one chance to be fully mindful about your growing baby. Stressing that you can't go back to your project or design when you're trying to comfort your baby won't help you deal with the situation at hand. Similarly, trying to come up with an effective baby-soothing strategy when you're working on a new marketing campaign will only limit your creativity. Try to be fully present with your baby when it's baby time, and fully focus on your work when it's business time. It might sound clichéd, but each moment—both in your baby and business life—will probably happen only once, so enjoy it while it lasts. Being in the moment is often all you need to prepare for the future.

It took me a while to adopt this approach to focus. Luckily, once I realised that letting go is the only way to go, everything started to fall into place. The best ideas for my business, including this book, came to my mind when I stopped worrying. Once I learned to focus on the task at hand—be it playtime, domestic chores, or business projects—without constantly thinking about my next move, new ideas and inspiration appeared in the least expected moments. Sometimes I had to quickly note down my thoughts to stop stressing that I would forget my new ideas. With a clear and worry-free mind, I was able to be fully present with my family. I practiced the same approach during my work—giving my full attention to my business during my work time created more space for better interactions and ideas during my family time.

Slowing down to speed up

Your career and business progress don't have to slow down when you become a mother. Although you'll probably have less time for professional development and for growing your business, this doesn't mean that a complete halt is the only option. The time you spend fully focusing on your child and family can be inspiring and enlightening, also in terms of your business. For example, by taking care of your baby, you'll eventually become more patient and more creative. You'll also learn to listen and talk in a more effective way while trying to understand and communicate with your child. These skills are essential to running a business and interacting with customers. You can become a better entrepreneur by being a good parent, and a better parent by being a good entrepreneur. These two areas do have a lot in common when it comes to social skills, negotiation, and management techniques. In my case, becoming a mother made me more confident and boosted my self-esteem in the business sphere. I stopped worrying so much about what other people might think or say about me and focused on what I needed to do. This helped me to become more effective and direct.

Slowing down to shape up

Taking it easy and reducing the number of items on your to-do list will also help reduce your stress levels. When you rush and experience stressful situations, your brain releases adrenaline, norepinephrine, and cortisol—hormones that temporarily increase your strength and focus. As a result, your blood is shifted to more essential areas such as your muscles rather than skin. These stress hormones also increase your blood pressure and make your breath shallower. While this "fight-or-flight" reaction can save your life when there's real danger (such as a car accident), prolonged periods of stress will have a detrimental impact on your physical and mental health. For example, constant surges of stress hormones can lead to heart diseases or weight gain because your body is trying to replenish the energy level that was used during the stress response. This process increases your appetite and stores more nutrients in the form of fat to prepare for the next energy-draining situation. High and repetitive stress levels also weaken your immune system, making you more susceptible to infections. What's more, chronic stress negatively affects your mental functions such as attention, concentration, and learning and memory, which makes you less intelligent and impact your decision-making skills. That's definitely too much to put at risk.

If you want to make sure your body and mind are fit enough to take care of yourself, your baby, and your business, you'll need to learn to slow down. Try to recognise what events, activities, or habits put your body in "fight-or-flight" mode so you can deal with your reactions effectively. Reducing sources of constant stress and learning to control your breathing will help you limit the negative impact of stress on your health. All in all, slowing down will calm your body and mind, creating a peaceful, more relaxed atmosphere in which you have more potential to thrive. This is essential, both in running your business and taking care of your baby. You need a clear mind to make the right decisions and come up with solutions to any problems you may encounter, and this will only be possible if you reduce the pressure in your life.

Slowing down to lighten up

Finally, if you associate the idea of a long break with boredom or fear of missing out, try to look at your maternity leave as a one-off gift. This is probably the only opportunity when you can fully take care of yourself and your child without any distractions and interruptions. After all, you get to be a first-time mum only once, so embrace it before rush hour starts again.

Getting used to the new order

Where am I?

Congratulations! After many months of intensive preparation you can finally hold your baby in your arms. There are many factors that can influence your mood and well-being now—the delivery you had, the hormones that are still at play, your surroundings, and your energy level. Every woman experiences childbirth in a different way, but there's something that unites us all: the variety of emotions that we feel when we become mothers. Joy, relief, disappointment, sadness, doubt, or anxiety—motherhood comes in many shapes and forms. During the first few months, frequent mood swings may be a part of your daily life, but all these changes and contradictory emotions are perfectly normal. This is the process of becoming a mother.

There's no need to feel guilty if your motherhood isn't always as joyful and sweet as it is often pictured in social and traditional media. Most women do feel extremely overwhelmed, nervous, or lost. In fact, about 15% of new mothers suffer from postpartum depression, and nearly every women experiences symptoms of the baby blues at some point after giving birth. As long as you can recognise if the situation gets out of control and seek help, you should be able to overcome even the darkest thoughts and the deepest anxiety. Talk about your feelings with your partner or friend, and don't hesitate to contact a professional therapist if you can't cope with your stress, nervousness, or disturbing thoughts.

The period following childbirth is so crucial that in many Asian and African cultures special arrangements are made to let the mother rest and nurture her baby while others take care of her. For example, in India, a new mother traditionally goes back to her own mother for six weeks after giving birth. In this way, a woman can give her full attention to her baby and focus on her own well-being. She is also relieved from all domestic chores and served food that supports recovery such as vegetable soups, porridge, ghee, cumin, almonds, fennel seeds, or aniseeds. Daily massages and tummy binding are also important practices that help to speed up the healing process. Such postpartum care puts the mother in a mentally comfortable zone and helps her rebuild her energy and bond with the baby.

When I found out about this approach, I tried to duplicate it in my life as much as possible. Although I wasn't able to move in with my mum for six weeks (we lived in different countries and my daughter had no passport), my parents came to visit us and stayed with us for one week to help around the house and with the baby. I practised belly binding and tried to massage myself and the baby nearly every day. A few weeks before delivery, I wrote a list of healing foods on a whiteboard in the kitchen to remind my husband what he should cook for us to support my physical and mental recovery. Apart from the right menu, we also made sure that I got enough warmth and rest. After giving birth, I stayed home for one week. During this week, I spent most of my time in my bed, although my home delivery had been prompt and unproblematic. This is how we managed to create a peaceful atmosphere to find the time and space for healing and bonding. Our home became our little sanctuary where everything was new, but everything was fine.

Unfortunately, the Western world often puts too much pressure on going back to normal in no time. Photos of celebrities spread across social media and articles in popular magazines or advertising campaigns keep promoting the race to get back—back to your pre-pregnancy body; back to your pre-pregnancy self. The main problem with this approach is that there's simply no way back.

As Kimberly Ann Johnson points out in her book *The Fourth Trimester*, after giving birth, you're always postpartum and you can never return to who you were before becoming a mother. Depending on the definition, the postpartum period can be anything between 10 days (the time needed for the uterus to go back to its normal size) to two years (the time recommended to start weaning). The healing process on the physical, mental, sexual, and emotional level could take months or years, depending on how you cope with this powerful transition. That's why it's unrealistic to expect to have, right after giving birth, the same body, the same mind, or the same level of performance in your business life as you had earlier.

There's no quick way to return to your old habits, behaviours, or reactions after the intense and transformative experience of childbirth. Even if you are ready to go back to your "normal life", including your work, chances are you won't be acting and thinking in the same way anymore. The changes around you and inside you might be subtle or drastic; you may or may not notice them, but once you become a mother, you will also become a different person.

Wherever you were in your business and private life before giving birth; there's no going back to that point. But that's not bad news. It's simply a unique opportunity to redefine yourself in each and every sphere—in your relationships with your family, your customers, and yourself. Try to look at it as a metamorphosis. You need to shed your old skin to make space for something new. It's a transformative process. And that's where you are right now.

Where is my mind?

With so many changes going on outside and inside your body, it's no wonder your mind begins to wander. The so called "baby brain" is a decline in cognitive abilities often experienced during pregnancy and shortly after giving birth. The exact reason for new mothers' forgetfulness and inability to focus during this valuable time is not yet known, but the most likely culprits are hormones, sleep deprivation, and stress.

Maybe the baby brain already became your daily companion during your pregnancy when you experienced moments of fogginess, forgetfulness, or a lack of focus. If you thought that your cognitive performance would go back to normal once your baby is born, I'll have to disappoint you. Your mind is also on a one-way journey on which (almost) nothing ever reverts to the starting point. Many women admit that they experience the symptoms of baby brain for up to two years after delivery. But even if your focus and attention improve over time, your priorities will probably change, and so will the way in which you act and respond to everyday challenges.

Your postpartum mind isn't your old mind. Switching back to work mode and running your business right after giving birth might not be an easy task. It's not only a matter of a lack of time, sleep deprivation, or poor physical well-being that can make your return to work complicated. Your work will also become more difficult because your mental resources now revolve around your baby and your new situation, whether or not you're aware of it.

It might feel like your brain is still on holiday, but there's no need to despair. If you really want to or have to return to your business immediately after delivery, there are several strategies that can help you manage your work better with your baby brain:

1. **Try not to take on urgent or overcomplicated tasks**
   Even if you feel ready for challenging projects, try to take it easy. Your body and mind are still going through a healing process. As you get used to your baby in the first few weeks, try to avoid stressful situations that will eventually reflect on your relationship with your child and other family members. For example, you might be tempted to accept a high-paying project with a short, same-day deadline. Even if your partner or someone else is going to watch your baby while you work, or you know you could complete the task during your baby's nap—don't assume that everything will run smoothly. What if your baby decides not to sleep at her regular time? What if your partner/babysitter/mother can't handle the baby if she suddenly becomes fussy and desperately wants to be back with her mum? Prepare a Plan B if you need to take on a rush job, and expect the unexpected. Alternatively, negotiate another deadline with your customer to be on the safe side.

2. **Notice when you perform at your best**
   If you're like most freelancers, you've probably noticed what the optimum time for you is to work or what types of surroundings help you focus the most. If you're like most mothers, your rhythm will probably change after giving birth. It will take some time before you settle into a new routine, but by observing your levels of energy, you'll be able to recognise the moments when you are able to work with the highest possible focus. Maybe it's during your baby's first nap. Maybe it's in the afternoon when your husband or partner comes back home. Or maybe it's right when you wake up and you can work

while someone else takes care of your baby. Maybe you are the queen of multitasking and are able to work even when your baby is awake. Your optimum time to work will depend on many factors, for example on the personality and health condition of your baby or on the amount of sleep you get at night. Try to figure out which part of the day is the most productive for you, and devote it to your business while making sure your baby is in safe hands.

3. **Add brain-boosting food to your diet**
A good diet can work miracles. Apart from including ingredients that support postpartum healing as mentioned in the previous chapter, you can also add products that are rich in good fats, antioxidants, minerals, and essentials vitamins that will improve your memory and increase your focus. Food with valuable brain power include fatty fish (like salmon), avocados, blueberries, walnuts, broccoli, turmeric, dark chocolate, or bananas. Of course, it will take some time before you see the results of a brain-boosting diet, so start adding these or similar products to your menu during your pregnancy already. The high levels of omega-3 contained in fatty fish will be also beneficial for the development of your baby's brain, so you can't go wrong with a brain-friendly diet.

4. **Make lists**
One of the easiest remedies to stop your brain from being forgetful is to create lists. If you can't remember what you planned to do in your work time or you feel overburdened with questions you want to ask your paediatrician or do research on, write everything down. If there's a risk that your list will get misplaced, use your phone to draft your notes. If you don't have time to type, simply record all your ideas, questions, problems

or thoughts on your phone. Just remember to come up with a clear naming convention when saving the recorded files so that you'll be able to find the right content when you need it. Searching through recorded audio may take longer than simply looking down at your handwritten or typed remarks, so another solution is to use mobile applications such as Evernote, Voice Assistant, Dragon Dictation, or Transcribe that convert voice to text. You can also use these apps for other tasks, like dictating your e-mails or marketing content for your business.

5. **Check and double-check**
Sleep deprivation, overwhelming emotions, uncertainty, and raving hormones can make you overlook little details or fall for hidden traps. If you feel that clumsiness has become a part of your daily life and you keep mixing up your e-mail recipients, failing to notice typos in your work, or misplacing items that you use very often, make a habit of double-checking everything—both in your work and when spending time with your family. For example, make an effort to focus on your wallet when you place it on a counter so you'll remember where to find it when you need it. Read your e-mails three times before hitting the send button. Whether you work with text, numbers, or visuals, try to spend more time on reviewing the quality of your work and verifying little details before handing your results to your customer. It may sound counterintuitive, as you probably feel that you have to work faster now rather than add extra steps to your work routine, but sometimes one more extra check is what makes the difference between a failure and success or between a happy and unhappy customer. Making sure your customers are still satisfied with your work, even if your brain is on

holiday, should rank high on your priority list, so try to be more thorough in everything you do.

6. **Take longer rest**
   The postpartum period is usually marked by high levels of fatigue. During the first few months after delivery, most women dream of being able to sleep more. You might think that it will take ages before you'll be able to get an uninterrupted eight-hours of sleep, but do try to get as much rest as possible. A well-rested mind and well-rested body are your key ingredients to smooth, effective, and pleasant interactions—both with your baby and your customers. It might feel tempting to fully maximise your baby's sleep time and devote it to work only, but after a few weeks of such a routine, you're likely to feel exhausted, depressed, helpless, or resentful. In such circumstances it's difficult to focus on nurturing your baby, not to mention delivering high-quality work. No matter how much caffeine or other boosters you decide to pour into your body, at some point you'll need to take a decent rest. Nothing will replace a good night's sleep, although it may sound like a luxury when your newborn constantly depends on you. To help your mind and body work more effectively, make sure you get a well-deserved rest at night or during the day. Sometimes an extra nap when your baby is asleep will be enough to recharge your batteries, and sometimes you'll need to ask your husband or other family members to let you sleep in while they watch the baby. With a relaxed body and mind you'll be more likely to tick off all those little things on your list and simply be fully present with your baby—when it's a family time—and your customers—when it's a business time. If you can't go to bed at a regular time and find yourself adding more housework and business activities at the end of the day, schedule your sleep time like you would any other activity. Make

a commitment to yourself that you'll be in bed every day at a certain time—10 pm, 11 pm or midnight—whatever suits your needs and is doable with your baby. Just make sure to follow the plan and get enough rest.

Where is my time?

No matter when you decide to resume your business, you'll quickly notice that your baby came with one more unexpected bonus—the ability to speed up time. With a newborn at your side, every day seems to whizz by, regardless of whether or not you're trying to squeeze in some work. Suddenly there's so much to do around the house and around the baby that you might forget about your own needs. Simply drinking a hot, freshly brewed cup of coffee might become a luxury—after taking one sip you rush back to your baby to entertain, feed, or change her, and before you know it, you're left with an ice-cold drink. When your baby is finally asleep, you try to read a few pages of a book, maybe even a short online article, only to doze off after a few seconds. The notion of time becomes vague and elusive during the postpartum period. Especially if, for the most part of the day, you're the only adult in the room.

If you're ready to go back to running your business immediately after the delivery, you'll probably need to manage your time in a better and more effective way than before. Ideally, a family member, childcare employee, or a baby sitter would stay with your baby regularly for a few hours per week so you can commit to your work without any interruptions. When this isn't an option or you simply want to devote as much time as possible to your baby, you'll need to redefine your work style and adapt to the new concept of time.

To manage your time more effectively when your days seem to be shorter and less predictable, you can use the following methods:

1. Apply Eisenhower's urgent/important principle

Try to categorise your tasks in four groups: 1) urgent and important, 2) important but not urgent, 3) not important but urgent, and 4) not important and not urgent. In this way you'll be able to determine which activities really require your attention and eliminate those that are merely distractions.

What are the important tasks? According to Dwight D. Eisenhower, former U.S. President who also served as a general in the US Army, important activities are those that lead to achieving our goals. Urgent activities, on the other hand, require urgent attention and are quite often related to someone else's goals. Usually we have to focus on these tasks as soon as possible, otherwise the consequences of neglecting them will be immediate.

So how can you use this principle in your business and private life?

1. List everything you feel you need to do, both in your business and family time.

2. Analyse each activity and assign it to one of the following categories:
1) important and urgent
2) important but not urgent
3) not important but urgent
4) not important and not urgent.

3. First, focus on the tasks in the first category. This could be items such as completing a project that is due today or sending your quote to a new customer. Then make sure you have enough time to carry out the items from the second category. You can schedule these activities for a particular time of day and then approach them with the

right level of attention. After all, these are the activities that will help you achieve your goals, so you should give them extra attention. These could include working on your long-term business strategy or developing a new online product.

4. Tasks from the third category—not important but urgent—are usually items that prevent you from achieving your goals. That's why you can easily delegate or reschedule them for another time. These could be tasks such as booking flights, answering certain e-mails, or scheduling social media posts—or other items that require your immediate attention but that you don't have to complete personally.

5. Finally, feel free to totally remove all the activities from the last category—these are only distractions, so you can cancel or ignore them with no remorse. Good examples of tasks from this category are browsing through social media and sorting your files or junk mail.

6. As a rule of thumb, always double-check if a particular activity is worth putting on the list in the first place. Try to avoid situations where other people dictate your priorities, or learn to say "no" in a polite way. This can often be your lifesaver and a guarantee of a (relatively) good night's sleep.

Now that you're both a mother and business owner, your time is one of your most precious resources. Try to be very strict when defining potential distractions and eliminating useless tasks. You might feel guilty after saying "no" repetitively to your friends, colleagues, or family members, but sometimes it's inevitable. To stay sane and be able to accomplish your goals, both in the family and business sphere, you'll need to set clear boundaries.

2. Try not to multitask

To make the best use of your time and brain power, it's important to only focus on one task at a time. This might seem counterintuitive, but multitasking really makes you less productive and is usually more time-consuming. Many studies have shown that our brain is not designed for heavy-duty multitasking. Switching from one activity to another actually costs us more time and energy than what we think we can save. Although the "switching costs" are as low as a few tenths of second, once you switch back and forth repeatedly over the day, this time quickly adds up. What's more, regularly switching between tasks also increases the chance of making errors, and the error penalties increase when the tasks are complex. Our brains simply can't do two things at the same time—you can't read and talk simultaneously, nor can you type or read at the same time. The only exception recognised in the research on multitasking is when you combine a very routine physical activity with a mental activity—such as walking and talking. However, some psychologists argue that even this combination isn't entirely possible and have proved that we miss many striking details when we combine such simple activities as walking and talking on a phone.

Multitasking takes a toll on your time, productivity, and energy, so do your best to get rid of this habit. Alternatively, you can find a golden middle ground and practise only "appropriate multitasking". Such a less harmful form of multitasking involves pairing mindless tasks with focus-dependent tasks. This could be, for example, walking with your baby in a stroller and taking a call or listening to inspiring podcasts while cleaning the house. Remember, however, that even with this mild form of multitasking, you'll probably fail to register some important details. If you feel stressed or under a lot of pressure when doing too many things simultaneously, simply put an end to it. You won't waste any time if you choose to focus on a single activity only. Quite the contrary—you'll benefit from it much more in terms of better focus and results.

If you tend to deal with several tasks simultaneously in your house and at work, try to stop for a while to see if anything changes. Analyse how combining two or more activities impact your mood, energy levels, and focus. If you can't imagine dropping the multitasking approach altogether, try to do only one thing at a time for at least one day. Do you feel equally drained as when you switch between several tasks? Do you think you've accomplished more? With what result?

I used to combine as many tasks as possible, thinking I could do more in a shorter time that way. I listened to my favourite podcasts when cleaning the house, I worked on several translation projects simultaneously, or constantly switched between marketing and performing my services, hoping that I could tick off more items from my list. In fact, I was only fooling myself. It was only when I made an effort to focus on one item at a time that I noticed I actually enjoy what I do. Being present and mindful helped me to notice more details and avoid many mistakes.

Unfortunately, my multitasking mode kicked in again when I became a mother. I tried to cook and entertain my baby simultaneously, but after a while I figured out that I can't focus on these two seemingly simple activities at the same time, and it simply made me feel rushed and upset. I also tried to listen to podcasts while putting my baby down to sleep, which often only required breastfeeding and hugging her until she closed her eyes. But after a few days, this approach made me feel like I was cheating my daughter and myself. One day, following the example of other freelance mothers, I also tried to work while watching my baby. I failed miserably. At some point, I realised again that multitasking doesn't work for me. It creates negative emotions and leads to poor results —not only when I work, but also when I spend time with my family or do housework.

Maybe you have a different approach or you can combine certain types of activities without feeling drained, stressed, or upset. Still, try to leave the multitasking approach for a while to see if a more focused strategy could be more beneficial.

Whether you pair physical and mental activities or focus only on one item at a time, make sure what you do is really beneficial to you and your baby.

3. Forget about perfection

Another approach that can hold you back is the constant strive for perfection. Sometimes perfectionism will help you achieve better results, but in most cases, it will become your obstacle to moving forward. With your busy business-mum schedule, you probably won't be able to complete every single house and business activity to the highest possible standard. There's simply not enough time in a day to perfect every single detail. Perfectionism can also stop you from trying out new things and make you procrastinate in your work and ideas.

Instead of aiming for perfection, choose to focus on consistency. For example, keeping to the deadlines agreed with your customers probably plays a key role in your business. If your client asks you to create a project proposal by Wednesday, submitting a perfect copy on Thursday won't be better than a good enough version that you deliver on time. Similarly, if you're expecting guests in a few hours but your house is a mess, your baby is fussy, and your customers are waiting for your response, you probably won't be able to welcome your visitors with a freshly baked cake and a shiny house. You'll need to set your priorities and get used to trade-offs. Good enough is sometimes good enough—you can't be a perfect mother, nor can you be a perfect business partner. But you can be good enough to meet the most important requirements and to make sure your family and customers are happy.

With a perfectionist mindset, you might easily procrastinate in your work or get stuck in analysis-paralysis mode. Sometimes you really just need to start somewhere, without waiting for perfect conditions. You can begin with what you have now and correct along the way if necessary. For example, you might be planning to create an online course to generate more income streams and position yourself as an expert. Your content is ready, but you are fixated on the ideal form. To achieve your dream result, you're convinced that first you'll need to invest in expensive equipment, develop superb editing skills, and find a breathtaking location to shoot your videos. You don't have any of these items yet, so you keep waiting until all the pieces of the puzzle fall into place. After six months spent on preparations, your course is still on the to-do list while others grab the opportunity and produce content on a similar topic without any fancy locations or top-notch equipment. Your time is your money, so sometimes you'll need to accept a reasonable compromise. If you're inspired and you feel you can inspire your students, maybe releasing the course in a not-so-perfect form isn't such a bad idea. You can always improve the published material or tweak it later in the process. In most cases, done is better than perfect, so try not to spend a lot of time on each and every project just to make it a little bit better. Is focusing on every little detail really worth it? What are you trying to achieve? Are the details you're obsessed with really essential to reach your goal?

Whatever you do, remember the 80/20 rule. This rule simply states that 80% of your outcomes come from 20% of your inputs. If you continue working on something to achieve 100% perfection, you might be using your time and energy in an inefficient way. Instead, consider investing these resources in an activity from the 20% category to get closer to your main goal.

4. Have a routine

A daily routine can be a real time saver for you, your baby, and your business. With an established schedule you don't need to improvise constantly or reinvent the wheel every single day. In this way, you'll save yourself from stressing about little things and have more energy and time for essential tasks. For example, you might begin every day at 7 am when your baby wakes up, then have a breakfast together, leave for a long walk, and come back home for your baby's nap so you can work on your projects while she sleeps. Then, in the afternoon, you can plan one more activity outside or do a bit of housework and playtime, eventually focusing on your work when your partner comes back home. Of course, your routine will heavily depend on your baby's needs and your family situation, and sometimes also on your financial means—such as being able to afford regular childcare for at least a few hours per week to fully focus on your business.

A daily routine, whether it's baby-led or parent-led or a mix of both, can help introduce some order in the chaos of motherhood as well as enforce your baby's development.

Your child will learn what to expect and won't be surprised or overly fussy when it's time to go out or when you need to work. You'll have more chances to predict when and for how long you can concentrate on your projects, and your customers will know when they're most likely to reach you. That's a win-win for everyone.

Establishing a routine with the newborn will take some time, but usually after two or three months you should be able to recognise common patterns in your child's behaviour. This is when most infants' sleeping and feeding habits become more consistent and predictable, so you might be able to adjust other activities to the rhythm of your baby. Of course, as your baby grows, the routine might change as well, so you'll need to be ready to tweak and adapt your schedule if you want to plan your day around your child's needs.

A routine is also good for your mental health and your business, especially during the first hours of the day. No matter what's going on around you, you need something that will help keep you sane. Your morning routine will prepare you for the day ahead, no matter what happened a day before or what is about to happen in the next few hours. Try to have at least a few minutes to yourself every morning, even if it means waking up before anyone else. Start your day peacefully with a coffee or a glass of water, shower, get some exercise in, do your affirmations or visualisations; anything that will help you keep grounded and focused. Regular habits and a relatively fixed schedule will also reduce your stress, both at work and at home, because you'll feel more in control.

5. Automate at home and at work

When you feel like motherhood eats too many of your minutes, you'll need an efficient way to save time and streamline boring and useless activities. This is where automation comes in. Think about your daily tasks as running a factory. Which processes can be automated or grouped into one slot to boost your productivity? For example, you could cook more food on a weekend and freeze extra portions for the following days to spend less time on preparing meals during the week. You could also run errands in blocks, combining grocery shopping with a visit to the local post office so that you don't have to go in the same direction twice. Maybe you have the option to shop online or shop for groceries once per week only. In this way, you can save quite a lot of time and money.

As I'm writing this book in April 2020, the coronavirus pandemic is sweeping across the globe. As it definitely forced many people and businesses to transform their daily activities, it also brought an opportunity to improve some aspects of our lives in the long run. One of my new habits is only buying groceries once per week. This does require some planning, but once you get used to it, you'll notice how much time and money you can save if you eliminate frequent visits to the supermarket, especially for items you don't necessarily need. I had planned to limit my trips to the grocery shop or switch to online grocery shopping long before the virus outbreak, but somehow the freedom to move around gave me exactly that—the freedom to decide when and for how long I could leave the house, even if it wasn't essential. Now, as many countries force their residents to stay home and eliminate non-essential activities, we discover that it is possible to live without some habits that used to form an integral part of our lives. Suddenly, many aspects of our lives have become automated to limit our exposure to potential infections.

Whether or not you changed your lifestyle during or after the pandemic, one lesson worth taking from this experience is that you can transform any habit, no matter how ingrained it is. Automating your tasks or doing similar tasks one after another is a good way to eliminate time-consuming processes and focus on what matters the most.

Bring this approach to your business as well. Automate as much as possible or combine similar tasks in one slot. Look at the tools you use at work—what can be done quicker and easier? Is your computer fast enough? Are your tools powerful enough to complete your work on time? Is there anything you can do to speed up your administration, accounting, or marketing? Automate tasks that are too time-consuming, such as issuing invoices manually, or delegate tasks that aren't your strong points. If you struggle with accounting or marketing, hire a professional to do it for you. It will save you a lot of time and energy that you can better invest in your core activities.

You can also start experimenting with tools that will limit your screen time or social media usage, if you discover that this is what distracts you at work. You can completely block Facebook, Instagram, or Twitter during specific hours when you need to focus on your work, or you can define how much time you'll spend on social media every day if you have to use these platforms for marketing.

Finally, if you struggle with focus or keep taking too many breaks, let automation take care of your workflow. Tools such as Tomato Timer will help you work using the Pomodoro technique: spend 25 minutes on work, followed by three to five minutes for a break. If 25 minutes seem too short to complete your project or any part of it, you can divide your work into 90-minute blocks. Again, there are tools that can help you establish such a method of working, or you can simply use your alarm clock to buzz every one and a half hour. With automated solutions you can track your daily habits to see what activities can be eliminated. For example, with RescueTime you can track time you spend on applications and websites to get an accurate picture of your day. With this insight, you can better structure your work and avoid unnecessary actions. If you feel you devote too much time and energy to any activity, experiment with tools that can help you manage your work better. Maybe consider using project management tools (such us Asana or Trello) or customer relationship management platforms (such as Bonsai, GSuite or HoneyBook), or invest in tools that are specifically designed for professionals in your industry.

With little tweaks here and there and with a couple of useful tools, you can boost your productivity and learn to work more effectively. You don't have to keep juggling and struggling, all you need is good preparation and a reasonable approach to your daily tasks.

What if I'm losing it?

Childbirth is a powerful experience. So powerful that sometimes it can turn your life upside down and make you walk in a direction you never thought you would take. For example, at some point after giving birth, you might lose your interest in your freelance career. You might shift your focus or feel that what you'd been doing earlier doesn't really matter. Especially if things don't go well in your industry or if you struggle to maintain your customer base. Maybe you don't feel like coming back to work at all, or maybe a silent voice inside of you tells you it would be easier to get hired and work for someone else, even if it's only part-time.

All these feelings of reluctance, lack of interest, or desire for a profound change are totally natural. Once you hold your baby in your arms and savour those moments of skin-to-skin contact, your priorities might begin to shuffle. This could be a temporary effect or the beginning of a long-term transformation. How do you recognise what the right step to take is?

To work or not to work?

Many mothers decide not to go back to work once their maternity leave is over. There could be a range of reasons behind this choice, but it's usually a combination of high childcare costs, long commuting hours, a desire to witness all the baby's milestones, and a lack of interest to go back to the "old life". Some mothers change their professional paths from being an employee to establishing a new business or from being self-employed to working in a company. Others decide to switch careers, whether as a freelance professional or an employee. There's no one ideal scenario when it comes to your postpartum work.

If you feel reluctant to go back to work after your maternity leave, you should analyse the situation before you make a decision. Consider whether what you're feeling is simply a temporary state of mind, probably influenced by depression, exhaustion, hormones, or health issues. Separate your emotions from your real desires to make sure you can make a conscious choice. First, crunch your numbers. If you can afford a longer maternity leave because you have a reasonable financial cushion or your partner's salary can cover your expenses, you'll be in a more comfortable situation to redefine your professional life or take a longer break. If you can't afford to stop working financially, you'll need to find a good solution.

Employed, self-employed, or a new self?

Spending a lot of time with your baby and being exposed to new experiences, problems, and behaviours can make your mind travel in previously unknown directions.

As your reality changes, so might your ambitions, aspirations, and preferences. For example, you may come to the conclusion that combining your freelance career with motherhood doesn't work well for you, no matter how hard you try. Maybe you can't focus anymore when you work from home, and sharing an office or working from a café generates too many costs. Maybe your salary doesn't cover the cost of childcare, or maybe you perceive your work to be more stressful than before. Maybe you come to the conclusion than continuing your business is not worth your time and energy anymore.

If you feel burnt out, this might be a good time to transform the way you work or tweak your products and services. For example, you could change the focus of your business, rebrand, or change your niche—as long as if feels right for you and for your family in the given moment. If you're fed up with developing mobile apps for your customers or writing content for their websites and would rather focus on your new passions—be it baby development, baking, or fitness—maybe you could turn your interests into a profitable business. If your heart lies somewhere else, figure out if you can switch your career or offer different services. Would you rather design baby clothes than logos and business cards? Are you tired of teaching yoga to adults and would prefer to teach kids only? Don't be afraid to take the first step in another direction if you're inspired by your new lifestyle. Motherhood can open up your mind to many fresh ideas, both in the professional and private sphere, so don't cling to your old habits if you feel disheartened. Just make sure that your business can still support you and your family if you need a regular and decent income.

No matter whether or how your approach to work has changed after giving birth, your decision to stay at home, switch your career, or rebrand doesn't have to be final. You can always come back to your initial business profile or abandon your freelance career for an employee life, if this is how you can improve your comfort and financial situation. There's no need to continue doing something that leaves you unfulfilled or doesn't meet your financial goals. It's never too late to adjust your professional life, yet none of your decisions have to be permanent.

Don't despair if you notice that you're losing your motivation or interest in your work. This is yet another component of your transition in the process of embracing your new reality. Sometimes becoming a mother will help you discover your real aspirations or give you energy to fully unlock your potential.

Is there anyone else?

Once the initial enthusiasm wears off and your hormone levels stabilise, you might start feeling another type of emotion: loneliness. If you chose to take maternity leave or reduce the scope of your business, you're bound to feel extremely lonely at some point. Even more so if your husband or partner leaves for work every morning. Spending a lot of time at home with your baby—whether you continue running your own business or not—will make you more likely to succumb to isolation and a lack of connection.

There are many reasons why mothers, especially first-time mothers, experience excruciating loneliness. First of all, your body has gone through enormous changes and needs a lot of time to recover. Usually it takes much longer than six weeks—the period that the Western world deems as sufficient to heal the wounds of childbirth and when the last postpartum medical check-up takes place. Depending on your delivery, your health condition, and your lifestyle as a new mother, your recovery can take a few months or even years. During the first weeks after giving birth, you will probably be in poor physical shape, which will decrease your energy to socialise with family or friends. On top of that, pregnancy and breastfeeding deprive your body of many valuable nutrients, so without a proper diet or supplements, your energy levels might drop even lower. Focusing on your baby, your recovery, and your business may further intensify your feeling of isolation. Socialising simply moves down on the priority list—whether you're aware of it or not.

Another factor that can contribute to your loneliness is the change in your routine. If you decide to work less or step down from running your business for a while, there will be fewer opportunities to interact with other adults—be it your clients, potential customers, colleagues, or business partners.

Staying at home and nurturing your baby might be energy draining. Sometimes it may seem that responsibilities related to your baby and housework never end. You can never tick off one task and consider it done because it comes back after a day or two—housework and baby work are iterative processes. That's why you feel there's always so much to do.

Even worse, your previous relationships may suffer as well—not only due to the lack of time but also due to the visible lack of connection between you and your friends who don't have children. As if all this isn't enough, the responsibilities of a new parent may follow you outside of home—so even if you do interact with your old friends and colleagues, it might not be the same type of connection anymore.

You might also feel distant from your husband. Bonding with your baby requires a great dose of energy and time, which might leave you feeling less inspired and enthusiastic to spend quality time together as a couple. No wonder you can end up feeling lonely even if you spend many hours with your partner in the same house.

There are others

Isolation might become a part of your new reality, but it doesn't have to stay this way. Prolonged periods of loneliness can influence the way you interact with your baby and your customers if you decide to go back to work immediately after childbirth. The worse and lonelier you feel, the bigger the influence your mindset will have on your baby. That's why improving your comfort level and mood plays such a crucial role. The first step you can take to leave the isolation behind is simply talking to someone else. This could be your partner, your best friend, your mother, your doctor, or your midwife. They might help you find the way out of your isolation or share their ideas and suggestions on how to enrich your daily life with more social interactions. It does take some courage to admit you can't cope with your new reality, but don't view your loneliness as a failure. It is just another inseparable component of your transition into motherhood.

What can you do to reconnect?

1. Join local groups for mothers

Do some online research or ask other mothers in your neighbourhood if they know of any clubs for mothers, baby cafés, or support groups for parents. Check your local library, places of worships, or city halls. Many locations run regular meetups for parents or new mothers, so ask around to find new opportunities to socialise.

2. Sign up to a class for babies and new mothers

Good places to meet like-minded women are postpartum yoga classes, swimming classes for babies, music lessons, or massage courses for babies and toddlers. Research online to find mum and baby activities in your neighbourhood or in your town. In most cases, you'll be surprised at how many opportunities there are to socialise while learning a new skill.

3. Connect via social media

If you lack the energy to go out or there seem to be nothing interesting going on in your area, you can start connecting with other mothers via social media. For example, there are plenty of Facebook groups for parents, first-time mothers, or self-employed mothers. You can join international, national, or local groups—it doesn't really matter, as long as you feel that the group members share similar problems and challenges. In this way you can find more ideas or simply engage with like-minded women. A local online community would also make it easier for you to meet new mothers face to face, for example in a baby-friendly café or in a park.

4. Reach out to your old friends

After giving birth, your relationships with your friends will probably change. For example, you may see your childless friends less often and spend more time with those who have kids. Maybe some of your friends don't want to disturb you in your busy new reality, and that's why they stop contacting and inviting you out. Don't wait for their messages or phone calls, simply reach out to them and suggest you catch up. If you're meeting your friends together with your baby, you probably won't be able to choose the same locations or activities you would have before you became a mother. However, you can easily find good alternative or child-friendly locations that could be pleasant for childless adults as well. Think about cafés with playing corners, a library with a children's section, parks, forests, or other natural areas. The rhythm of such meetings will probably be dictated by your baby's behaviour, but nothing is impossible. You can still enjoy your time with your friends if you prepare yourself and your baby for nearly every possible scenario, such as breastfeeding, diaper changes, or playtime.

5. Find groups for business/freelancing mothers

If you continue to run your business immediately or shortly after giving birth, you might think you have absolutely no time to socialise with other parents. Especially if most of the women you meet online and offline are on a paid maternity leave or chose to be stay-at-home mums. You might also notice that you can't really connect with mothers who focus on only their children without the need to squeeze in some precious work around their baby's schedule. Still, don't let this become a reason to neglect your social interactions. An alternative to joining a typical mothers' group could be a community for self-employed mothers. Find such groups online or connect to other business mothers via social media. For example, you can use specific hashtags on Instagram (such as #selfemployedmum, #mumsinbusiness, #freelancingmum) to have a peek into the lives of other freelancing mothers and interact with them. Maybe there are other business mothers in your area. If there's no local meetup for business mothers, maybe you can set it up. For example, you can start by building an online community and then move the interactions to real life. This will give you more opportunities to share your struggles and rewards but also to motivate and support one another.

Connecting with at least one group or signing up for just one class can bring more joy and purpose to your daily life. It will make you feel more motivated to leave the house and look at your problems and challenges from a different perspective.

Like most new mothers, I felt completely abandoned during the first few weeks after giving birth. I craved to have my old, quite busy and social life back, but I knew this wasn't an option anymore. That's why I began an intensive search for anything baby and mother related that my city (Amsterdam) and my neighbourhood had to offer. I signed up for a postpartum yoga course, a baby massage class, a baby swimming course, and baby sensory classes. Most of these activities are for babies that are at least six weeks old, so before my child reached this long-awaited milestone, I also registered at the local library and soon discovered a free meetup group for parents in a nearby school. As I was also trying to run my business, all these meetups quickly started to eat too much of my energy and time. After a while, I had to reduce and reorganise my social activities, but meeting other mothers and learning new skills definitely helped me to feel more alive and less isolated. The courses and classes I followed were also a good source of inspiration on how to spend time with my baby at home.

If you don't live in a big city and there are no local groups and classes for new parents nearby, maybe you can start your own meetup. Advertise via social media or in a local library, and soon you'll notice that you're not the only mother looking for more opportunities to leave the house.

Your family is there

Being self-employed and tending to your baby may become extraordinarily hard if there's no one around to support you. Add to that the pressure—from the outside world or from yourself—of running a household, and you can end up with an impossible juggling act. That's why you need to learn to ask for help, both in your business and private life. You simply don't have enough time nor energy to deal with everything alone, even if you think you can cope. No matter how strong or motivated you feel, sooner or later your mind and body will fail to support you in this tough race. If you usually prefer to wait until someone spontaneously offers to help you, this is the right time to quit waiting and learn to be more direct. People around you might be too busy, too focused on their own world, or simply too shy to lend a hand. That's why speaking your mind and requesting the help you need is the first step to avoiding many unpleasant surprises. It will also take a great weight off your shoulders.

Yes, you can do it all alone, but there's no point in being stubborn and acting like you're strong and independent—even if you really are. This was my approach at the beginning, but it quickly left me terribly overwhelmed and exhausted. I made the mistake of not asking my husband for help often enough. I would just run the errands and do the growing pile of housework while entertaining our baby, even when my business projects were piling up as well. I remember one particular Sunday in the first month of my motherhood: I went out for an extra-long walk with our daughter so that my husband could work on his music project without interruptions and volume limitations. I did this voluntarily, even though I felt like we should actually switch roles so that I could finally work and rest after a tiring week. I was our baby's sole carer from Monday to Friday, every day for at least 10 hours a day while trying to learn how to be a mum and keep running my business. On that Sunday in November I chose to have a happy husband while being slightly upset myself. I preferred this option over the reverse situation—where my husband would be upset due to a lack of time for his hobbies and side projects, but I would finally have had time to rest or give more attention to my business. At the end of the day, this option would probably have made me feel much more frustrated, and a very frustrated mum often means a very frustrated baby. I chose to sacrifice my time and energy just to make sure everyone else was happy.

All in all, I didn't demand much. I learned to stretch my time and silently continued working on my business when our daughter was asleep, including on the weekends. Luckily, this situation didn't last long, and after five months I finally learned to ask for help to be able to better organise my schedule, my priorities, and caring for our baby.

You can make it all alone, but you don't have to. Your family and friends are there to support you. Sometimes all you need to do is to clearly say what you expect them to do. After all, asking for help is a sign of strength, not a sign of weakness.

You are here too

Feeling lonely or isolated can also have an impact on how you treat yourself. Neglecting your own needs can further intensify your lack of connection with the outside world and with your real self. Your business and your baby need the best version of you—as relaxed as possible, motivated, taken care of, physically and mentally strong. This is not an easy feat, especially if your responsibilities seem to multiply and your to-do lists never end. Still, your self-care should be your priority. Even if it means working less in the evening to get more hours of sleep or asking someone to stay with your baby while you finally have your hair done, go to a gym, have a long walk alone, or do just about anything that will put your mind and body back into balance.

Lie down and meditate, read a book, or do anything else that will help you connect with yourself. Put aside the housework, delegate some tasks that you think can be carried out only by you, and let go of the race. No matter how overwhelmed you feel, remember to schedule some time for yourself. As little as 15 minutes per day spent on your needs will help you find more energy and motivation to move forward. Look after yourself physically—this means eating nutritious food, resting when you can, and doing mild or moderate exercise. Sneak in some moments of mindfulness by doing only one thing at a time and fully embracing the activity at hand. In this way you can clear your mind and remind yourself that you're not only a mother. There are so many other roles you play in your life: you are a wife/partner, business owner, daughter, friend, dog-lover/yogini/musician (or insert anything else that applies to you). Don't let motherhood completely take over your life. It's not a selfish concept. It's an important step to keep your sanity and some degree of balance.

If you're struggling with feelings of guilt whenever you take time off from mothering, doing housework, and running your business, maybe one of these methods will help you embrace the idea of self-care:

1. Every time a negative thought appears telling you to stop or rush with your self-care rituals, try to beat it and overwrite it with positive thoughts. You can close your eyes, take a deep breath, and repeat phrases such as "My rest benefits my baby and my business. I need to take some time off to be a better mother and business owner." It might seem silly at the beginning, and you might feel it's not effective at all, but after a few attempts, you'll learn to slow down to attend to your own needs.

2. If one hour spent on exercising, reading a book, or catching up on sleep seems like a total waste of time to you, break it down into pieces. Start with small steps, for example, commit to 10 minutes of you time per day. This time should be filled with activities fully focused on you—a long relaxing bath, stretching, massaging your body, or doing anything else that will make you feel and look better. Yes, you could theoretically squeeze in so many other important tasks in these 10 minutes, such as

writing, translating, designing, or marketing your services. But what quality will your work be if you're dead tired? How much energy will you have for your baby if you keep forgetting about yourself? Ten minutes of restoring relaxation and focusing on only yourself only might be all you need to boost your mood, productivity, and motivation for other important tasks.

3. If you think that resting and taking extra care of yourself is a waste of time, experiment for one week to see how the time invested in self-care changes your mood and attitude towards your work and your baby. Try alternating between different types of activities such as one extra hour of sleep, 10 minutes of reading, meditating, or yoga. Then, on another day, fill your schedule with other to-do tasks as you usually do, with no or very limited time for yourself. At the end of each day analyse your mood, your productivity levels, and motivation. Did you really get more quality work done when you rushed and skipped an opportunity to do something good for your mind and body? How patient are you with your baby if you don't have time to reconnect with yourself? Which version of yourself do you prefer—the one that can stop the race to tune in or the one that constantly keeps ticking off the tasks centred around the house, baby, and business?

Treating your self-care as a priority rather than an afterthought doesn't mean that you'll neglect your baby and your work. You don't need to take one or two hours for your wellness every day. As little as 10 minutes can do wonders, as long as you truly commit to it and use this time to restore your energy by doing something that you enjoy.

How can I stay on top of it?

To make the best use of your limited time as a self-employed mum, you'll need much more than good time-management skills, a supportive family, or a rested mind and body. There are two more factors: focus and motivation.

Let's assume you've already found a way to work around your baby's rhythm or you have access to affordable childcare. What if feelings of guilt consume you every time you spend a few hours on your work rather than playing with your baby? What if your thoughts constantly go to your baby's milestones or health issues, and every time you sit down to work you end up googling tips on how to make your baby sleep better, cry less, eat more, or survive teething pain? Quite often, the time you have allocated for running your business might be marked by a fierce fight between you as a businesswoman and you as a mother. So, how can you redirect your thoughts back to the task at hand and leave the maternity concerns for later?

Realign and refocus

One good method that helped me stop my thoughts from running to my baby whenever I worked was to write down any idea or any concern that crossed my mind. For example, if I knew I had only three hours per day to complete my translation projects and do a little bit of marketing before the babysitter's shift finished, I would shut myself in my home office, put on my headphones, and switch to my work zone. Any time my mind told me that I was neglecting my baby or that I should do some research on her sleep patterns or find some more clothes for her online, I'd simply add a new task to my to-do list. I kept reminding myself that this was valuable and unique work time. The music I listened to helped me to block out all the surrounding noise, so I didn't hear my baby even though she was in a room just 15 meters away from me. Whenever my focus dipped using this technique or I needed to extend the distance between me and my baby or my house to be more focused on my work, I'd go to work in a nearby café. That often meant that I would have 10 minutes less to finish my business projects, and I would have to work on a laptop, which I truly dislike doing. But giving up the comfort of working from my cosy office with its ergonomic keyboard and two large screens to move to a tiny and inconvenient café table with other freelancers typing next to me would sometimes magically boost my productivity. Plus, one visit in a café would usually make me appreciate the perfect working conditions I had built at home throughout the years. A little change of surrounding was sufficient to motivate me in the long run.

Every time your mind drifts away when you should be focusing on the task at hand, try a similar approach. Write down or record what bothers you on your phone. Give your thoughts some tangible form and put them aside for later. Then go back to your work. If this doesn't help, change your environment. A major obstacle for freelancers working from home is the fact that they work from home. You don't need to invest in a co-working space or a fancy office, all you need is a separate workspace, even if it's located in your home. Stop working at your dining table, dressing table, or on a sofa with your laptop on your knees. Do your best to arrange even the tiniest corner in your house into a comfortable and productive working area. Working around other people—in a café or library—can also have a positive impact on your focus and motivation. Plus, it will give you opportunity for more social interactions, which plays a crucial role in your well-being.

Finally, think about strategies you used to focus before you became a mother. What used to motivate you to complete your business tasks? What helped you focus? If a cup of coffee, jogging, or meditation doesn't work for you anymore, or you simply don't have the option to continue with your pre-motherhood rituals, find a new, quick routine that will help you instantly switch to work mode. For example, if you're busy with your baby and household all day long and squeeze in your work during your baby's sleep time, think of some transition ritual to get in the right frame of mind. Every time you leave your baby sleeping in her crib and move towards your workstation, brew a fresh cup of coffee, fill your glass with water, or close your eyes and take five deep breaths. This short routine will help you smoothly move from one activity to another. If you do it regularly, your routine will quickly switch your mind into the right mode—boosting your focus and motivation. You can also introduce another ritual at the end of your work time to quickly transition into mothering mode again. This will help you have more enthusiasm for the daily grind, even if the time allocated for your business tasks seems exceptionally short.

Remove and replace

Sometimes achieving a better level of concentration and boosting your enthusiasm for work won't be possible until you completely eliminate all sources of distraction and disturbance. Start with your workspace. Can you quickly get down to business when you reach your desk? Do you need to clean up crumbs and remove empty glasses before you can focus? Make sure your work area is decluttered every time you enter it. A tidy and clean workspace will put your mind at ease. On the other hand, a disorganised desk will make your brain cluttered and chaotic. Even if you don't consider the clutter to be a major disturbance to your productivity, your brain does notice it and adjusts to your surroundings accordingly. Try making your space as minimal and as clean as possible to see if it changes the way you feel and the way you work.

If you don't have a spare room to use as your home office and your only option is to work in a designated corner somewhere, make sure it's not a bedroom. Your mind will automatically switch to rest and relaxation, making it more challenging for you to focus on being productive. Also, when you later go to sleep in the room where you worked, you might have problems falling asleep.

To further eliminate potential distractions, you can arrange your workspace so that it faces a wall or a window. There shouldn't be too many objects in your field of vision, for example a messy room or busy street, as this will decrease your brain power. Make sure the space in front of you is simple and balanced to help you concentrate on what matters the most.

If you struggle to keep your wandering mind on track, it might be a sign that you need a better source of energy. Our thoughts usually drift away if there's not enough power for the brain to function properly. The brain's neurons need energy to continue working, and if they lack glucose and glycogen, their capacity—thus also our mental power—will be reduced. That's why you need a healthy diet that can quickly deliver the required energy to your brain. Take another look at the "Where is my mind" chapter to find out what products can help you increase your focus.

Even with a healthy diet and a clean workspace, you might still notice your thoughts wandering. If you tend to daydream or stress too much, but would rather concentrate on your work, set an alarm for two or three minutes to allow yourself to sink into daydreaming for this limited period only. Once the alarm goes off, come back to your task and don't let your focus shift anymore.

What if you still can't control your distracting thoughts? What if your work time becomes "baby problems research time" more often than you'd like it to be? What if you keep searching for inspiration for your next marketing campaign instead of completing your urgent and important tasks? Pay attention to what triggers your mind to wander. Maybe it's social media, maybe a picture of your family that you've put on your desk, maybe a beautiful painting with a beach on your wall, or maybe the sound of your baby coming from another room. Any time you notice that you're thinking about something other than your work, try to define what happened immediately before your mind drifted away. Locate that disturbing factor and eliminate it.

Finally, remove all the distractions of your phone and social media. Put your phone in silent mode and close all the social applications. If you need social media for your work or to communicate and engage with your customers, set time limits to avoid wasting valuable minutes. Another option is to take advantage of tools designed to control the way you use social platforms or simply make a deal with yourself that you will only hang out on Facebook or Instagram for 20 minutes per day, and only for business purposes.

Sometimes, no matter what you do, you won't be able to turn your work mode on. To flip the switch, try dropping the task you're stuck on and start somewhere else. For example, if you design or write in a linear way, move a few steps forward and work on another bit of your project. Then come back to where you left off to finish the challenging piece. If your deadline is not pressing, maybe you can leave the unfinished task for another day when your focus will be back in its place. Maybe your mind is simply telling you to take a break or a short nap. Listen to your body to make sure you don't drain your physical and mental power.

To realign and refocus, you need to remove distractions from your environment and workspace and replace them with things that inspire enthusiasm and increase your concentration levels. Regardless of the methods you choose to unplug yourself from your "mothering side" and connect to your "business side", remember why you started. Why did you choose to be self-employed, and why do you want to continue now that you're a mother? This quick introspection should give you a huge motivation boost to complete even the most tedious task.

What if there's a cloud on the horizon?

Being a freelancer means that you are in full control of whether and how your business prospers. To make sure you're not only keeping your business afloat but also thriving and heading in new directions, you can expand your streams of income and create an emergency plan.

If you haven't done so already before your pregnancy, now is the ultimate time to prepare for potential trouble, business stagnation, or economic recession. Apart from having an appropriate financial buffer, as discussed in Chapter 1, it's also important to secure a steady profit without the constant exchange of your time and skills. Your small business is very likely to be affected by events occurring in your direct and indirect surroundings, such as political reforms in your country, epidemics that paralyse the global and local economy, or new policies and standards in your industry. To protect yourself and your business from such adverse effects, you should start generating passive income.

Keep a cool head

No matter what industry you work in, there's always something you can share with others—such as your knowledge and experience—and convert into a steady source of income. For example, you could create an online course based on your area of expertise. If you're a freelance photographer, maybe you can teach others how to take specific types of pictures. If you're a graphic designer, maybe you can show people how to use a certain tool or find inspiration for amazing designs. The possibilities are endless. If you think that you don't have enough skills to actually create a course, don't worry. There are online courses on this topic as well. You don't need to spend a big sum on learning how to create a course or on the actual course development. It will take some time to set up good-quality content, especially if you choose to do all the steps by yourself—from creating the slides through recording to editing—but in most cases, it's worth the effort. Your digital product will be delivered automatically once it's recorded and hosted on your website or on a teaching platform, so you won't have to only sell your time and skills for every cent you make. Of course, you'll need to learn how to promote your course, but the more students you have and the more courses you create, the smoother and quicker the whole process goes. Online courses are an excellent source of passive income if your content is relevant and up to date.

My adventure with passive income begun in 2014 when I created my first online course. I enjoyed all the technical aspects of this process, probably more than the actual teaching. Editing, recording, preparing the materials—I was fully responsible for every single step in creating my first two courses. Maybe the quality wasn't top-notch, maybe some details could have been more polished, but at the end of the day, what really matters is that you have engaging and valuable content. Besides, these courses were very niche (website and mobile application localisation for translators), so once the lectures were published, the number of students started to grow rapidly. The only mistake I made was the teaching platform I chose to host my products on. Without giving it too much thought, I simply picked a service that inspired me to create my own course and which was extremely popular at that time. This choice wouldn't have been that bad if I had invested more time and skills in promoting my products to limit the platform's commission. Otherwise, if all the traffic and sales is generated by the hosting platform only, you can end up with a ridiculously low cut. Eventually, my courses did become a decent source of passive income, but not as significant as I had planned it to be. Luckily, the real adventure began when I integrated the courses with my own website through another, more professional service provider.

If you're thinking about creating an online course as well, don't fall into the trap of copying the ideas, tools, and processes of other online instructors. There's never one right way of teaching online or promoting your content. If you want to design a successful course, you'll first need to do thorough research to find out what the pros and cons are of every tool or marketing strategy that you want to implement. Take some time to decide where to host your content, how to promote it, and how to approach your target audience. This will require some initial work, but once everything is set up, all you need is regular maintenance to keep your products engaging.

Another way to ensure a constant flow of income is to use affiliate marketing or sell spaces on your blog. There are companies out there that need the support of influencers and bloggers. That's why they pay for sponsored articles or offer other incentives to mention their products or services. If your blog or social media profile is popular, you could turn that into a money-making tool by helping other businesses promote their products.

Another idea is to share your expertise in the form of an e-book and then promote it to your target audience. You can do this instead of developing online courses or as an addition to such products. If you think that there are already many other more popular authors or many other books about your chosen topic, remember that everyone has a different story to tell. Your experience and personality are unique. If you let it shine through your content, there really is no competition at all.

Finally, nearly every industry has specific ways of generating passive income. For example, many website developers create website templates—for WordPress or Drupal—and then sell their products to multiple users, often with additional long-term services such as technical support. If you're a graphic designer, you can develop usable templates for social media posts, brochures, or business cards, and then offer your products for sale to many different customers. If you're passionate about writing and have an interesting story to tell, consider writing and self-publishing books. This can be another great source of income, as long as you make sure your books are promoted in the right way and to the right audience.

With reliable passive income you will be financially prepared for any limitations and obstacles that can occur in your personal life and in your work environment. Sometimes, however, you'll need much more than a constant flow of income.

Weather the storm

Generating multiple streams of income for your freelance business might not be enough to prepare for a potential emergency. A financial buffer is only one of many ingredients to a recipe for success.

Once you become a mother, it's time to reassess your and your business's condition. First, do a quick brainstorming session with yourself or with someone you trust. What can happen in your personal and business life that might prevent you from working? What could put your business on hold?

Below are some examples of situations you might want to consider when creating an emergency plan:

1. Your regular customers stop working with you or go bankrupt.
2. Your children get sick and you have to stay home or accompany them in hospital.
3. You lose your main childcare provider (babysitter, family member, day care).
4. You need to limit your work activities due to a serious epidemic or new policies in your country.
5. A law regulating freelance activity changes to your disadvantage.
6. You need to take a break from work due to an illnesses or short-term disability.
7. Your customers sue you because they're unhappy with your work.
8. You burn out and can't cope.

This list is by no means definitive, so take some time and analyse how your business functions to define more situations that could put your business and life at risk. Think about events that scare you the most or circumstances that would leave you helpless. Next, come up with effective strategies to prevent or overcome every single event on your list.

For the situations described above, some effective solutions could include the following:

1. Diversify your offer and your customer base so that your income doesn't rely on one regular customer and one service. Make sure to network in the online and offline world even when everything is going well. Remember to promote your services or send out regular newsletters to your existing customers to remind them about your business. You can consider launching a free e-book to bring more leads to your

173

ecosystem, host podcasts, organise webinars, or write a blog to always remain visible and have a stable audience. There are many ways to add more variation to your services and marketing strategy. Choose methods that work best for you and activities that you could add to your already-busy schedule.

2. If you need to fully focus on your children's well-being, make sure you have someone who could temporarily take over your business. Try to arrange good health insurance for yourself and your children to avoid high healthcare costs. Another strategy is to always have a safe financial net or generate a decent passive income that will cover your expenses if you need to take a longer break.

3. Again, make sure your business can function to a limited degree even if you can't give it your full attention. If there's no one else to watch your baby while you work, you might need to resort to "baby nap working mode" and carry out your business tasks only when your baby is sleeping. Prepare a list of alternative childcare providers, for example other babysitters or family members, in case you can't rely on your regular solution.

4. This is where passive income and your financial cushion comes in. That is, as long as the pandemic or new policies don't affect your passive streams of income. Every scenario is possible, as we experienced during the outbreak of Covid-19, so don't take anything for granted.

5. Make sure you know whom to contact for legal advice. Regularly work with the same legal advisor who knows your business and the legal environment

in your country to support you accordingly. To get ready for any potential legal hurdles, make sure you know what the requirements would be if you were to change your business's legal structure, if that's the only way to run your business more smoothly. Sometimes governments decide to regulate certain professions, for example, by requiring an industry-skills certificate. What would you do if such a law was introduced in your country? Do you know what to do to have your skills certified? If you already have such a certificate but you obtained it in another country, do you know how to make it valid and recognised in your country of residence?

6. Disability insurance, passive income, and a decent financial cushion will be your saviours when your health deteriorates. If you haven't done so already, make appropriate arrangements to be ready to withstand any major health crisis.

7. Nobody is perfect, and receiving a bad feedback from time to time isn't the end of the world. However, you need to have a system in place for dealing with unhappy clients. For example, make sure you always understand all requirements, sign an agreement with your clients, or make them accept your terms and conditions. Before the situation escalates, find out how to solve your client's complaint. Maybe you can redo your work or offer a discount for a future project. If all your strategies fail and the customer decides to sue you, you'll need adequate insurance. Otherwise, as a solo trader, you might end up risking your entire livelihood. Professional liability insurance will help you protect yourself and your family against claims for damages from third parties.

8. Running a freelance business and taking care of your baby might leave you feeling overwhelmed and exhausted. In extreme cases, you could also experience burnout or lose interest or motivation in your work. The best approach to prevent this from happening is to take regular breaks, pay more attention to your self-care and well-being, and ensure that you implement the necessary changes to your private and business life to reduce stressful factors. Make a list of things that improve your mood and help you reset. You'll need it once you recognise any physical or emotional signs of burnout. Also, make sure there's someone you can talk to if you notice that you can't cope with your work or your responsibilities.

Managing your private and business life is like managing a complex project. All good project managers know that to launch a project, you first have to identify the key risks. The next step is to come up with strategies to mitigate any potential problems. Write down the obstacles you might encounter during your projects and develop action plans to deal with them. Then, once you find yourself in tricky situations, you'll be able to turn things around without stressing too much and hectically searching for effective solutions.

Where shall I go?

If you spend too much time with mothers of children older than yours, you might be surprised at how much free time these women have. They don't need to constantly breastfeed or hold their kids in their arms, and they don't need to sing songs to them when they cook or drive to provide a decent level of distraction and entertainment. They don't have to accompany their child on every single step. They can leave their six-year-old with a pile of toys and have some time for work. If a child is at school already, a mother can spend as much as six hours on her business without splashing out on day care or a babysitter. What a luxury!

Or is it?

Before my daughter was born, my friends and family kept telling me that once I survive the first year, everything would be easier. Once I made it through the first year in one piece, other business mothers kept repeating that everything would be better once my child starts school. In my mind, school became this magic solution that would instantly solve all my problems. It would bring me more freedom, more work time, and longer periods of rest. Suddenly, I'd be able to focus on my tasks and grow professionally without any interruptions. I would even be able to leave the house for several hours or have my "old life back".

There I was, waiting impatiently for the first year to finish and then for the first school year to come, hoping that this new phase would reward me for my hard work.

Until I took a closer look at this image and noticed that it was nothing more than an illusion.

The blurry image

Yes, chances are you'll have more time for yourself and your business when your child leaves the intense babyhood stage. And yes, your child will become more independent at some point and let you sleep longer on the weekends. But with school comes new responsibilities and new challenges, both for you and your baby. Suddenly, you might find yourself running around the park at night trying to find chestnuts that your child needs for her art class the next morning and forgot to tell you about until just before going to bed. Or you'll end up fighting the morning madness, trying to get your child ready for school on time. Or you'll stress that taking and picking up your kids from school always takes so much time. Not to mention the never-ending errands for school supplies, books, uniforms or after-school activities. Even if your child spends about six hours per day in class, it's not as long as you might think it is. Especially if you also need to squeeze in some non-business-related tasks in your short day. Responsibilities such as driving your children to school and picking them up, answering "urgent" e-mails from teachers and school organisations, and getting ready for school events and special days might slash your "business-only time" by half.

The distant future

Don't delay your personal and business growth until the day your children finally go to their first class. Don't wait for school to save you from exhaustion and grant you more time to work. The years that follow may or may not be easier for you and your family, but there's no need to keep procrastinating and leaving your business ideas for later. If there's anything you want to modify and reshape in your freelance career, do it now or as soon as you can. Assign a deadline to your goal, and stick to it.

Running a freelance business and being a parent is a lifelong learning process. It's not a task you can simply tick off and move on. If you want to do it quite well, there will always be something to change, upgrade, remove, enhance, or let go. That's why it's wise to add your professional and personal development to a to-do list or include it in your annual growth plan. Once per year or once per month, jot down the skills you want to learn, the courses you want to follow, the books you want to read, and the goals you want to achieve. Even if you think there's no space for you to grow and you merely have energy to keep your head above water, make the effort to plan your progress. It's easy to get caught up in the daily grind, racing against the clock. But from time to time try to take a deep breath and figure out if what you are doing now will help you move closer to where you want to be in the future, both in your private and professional life.

The first year of combining your motherhood with running your business might leave you breathless. Eventually, you might be forced to push your work lower down the priority list. But when the storm settles down, try to look at the not-too-distant future more clearly and decide how you want to move on with your business, your parenting skills, and yourself. Just don't let that storm last for too long, and don't assume that your life will start only when your child becomes older.

When new opportunities arise

Thriving in your business

Once you've made it through the first year of motherhood, give yourself a pat on the back. If you tried to run your business during this time as well, give yourself another one. You've made it through what's considered the toughest time in the life of a first-time mother!

To say that from now on everything in your family and business will be painless is an overstatement of the century. Every year and every milestone of your baby's life comes with its own challenges. Even though you've made it through the peak of sleep deprivation, this is just the first step on a long journey of self-discovery and adaptation. You've probably gone through a profound transformation already and are now a stronger, more confident woman. Motherhood changes your personality. Whether you're aware of it or not, you're not the same person anymore. Every revolution devours its children. In this case, your mind, body, and personality were transformed by your pregnancy, delivery, and motherhood. But every revolution also brings new opportunities. It's time to look around and dive inwards to take advantage of your new reality.

New person, new business

Research tells us that a mother isn't the same person she was before giving birth. For example, Dutch scientists recently proved that during pregnancy, foetal cells enter and travel through the mother's entire body. From a biological perspective, the presence of cells with a different genetic makeup in your body confirms that you're a different person.

But you don't need research to realise this—look at your family members and friends who became mothers to notice this change. Or dive in and explore how you've transformed since becoming pregnant and giving birth. African cultures have a long-cultivated belief that mothers and their babies form one unit, hence the word "mamatoto" that describes this inseparable integration. A mother and her baby are connected on a physical, psychological, energetic, and spiritual level. Although this interdependence may weaken after the first few months, the bond is still there, and that's one of the factors that contributes to your personality change.

As you learn new skills and realign your priorities during the first year of motherhood, you also create another version of your freelance business. Chances are that taking care of your child has taught you how to be more patient, more assertive, and more confident. Maybe you notice that you don't care so much about what other people think or say about you anymore because what really matters is the safety and health of your family. You might also have learned how to be quicker and better at solving problems and making crucial decisions. All these skills are very useful in business, so take advantage of the new version of yourself. For example, if your motherhood boosted your self-esteem, bring this confidence to your communication with your customers or potential clients. Do what you've always planned to do but kept procrastinating and believing that you lacked the skills required to take the first step. Start that e-mail marketing campaign, create a shiny social media profile, keep following up with your leads, be active at networking events—you probably now have the courage and social skills to achieve those scary business goals.

Maybe the way you communicate has changed as well—when talking to toddlers you need to be as clear as possible before their attention diverts. Try to keep the same clarity and simplicity when dealing with your customers, and your collaboration will become much smoother and easier.

In my case, the first year of learning how to be a good mother and leading by example rather than instructions definitely improved my business relationships. There's no time to waste for lengthy explanations, introductions, or descriptions. The time to grab your potential client's attention—be it online or offline—is severely limited, so you need to get straight to the point. On the other hand, learning how to set boundaries with my child allowed me to be more assertive with my customers. Sometimes some requests are impossible to fulfil, and some deadlines can't be met. Before my pregnancy, I would often accept projects that were nearly impossible to complete, but once my priorities changed, I finally learned to say "no". Negotiating with my daughter helped me to negotiate better with my clients to reach more beneficial collaboration terms and eventually have more quality time for my family.

Take a few moments to analyse how your behaviour and actions may have changed after so many months of being a mother. There must be something you can take advantage of and transfer to your business life. Maybe it has happened already, but you're not aware of it.

New environment, new connections

Another way in which motherhood will help you grow your business is the change of environment. Your late birthday parties will probably now be replaced by early morning kinder balls, and your business networking events will be replaced by mum-and-baby activities. These are also great opportunities to learn and grow, both in the private and business sphere.

By attending yoga or swimming classes with your baby, joining clubs or cafés for parents, or simply chatting with other parents on a playground or at a birthday party, you're expanding your network. These new connections may or may not result in paying customers, but you'll definitely be able to spread the word about your products and services. So don't refrain from talking about your job or professional life in child-centric environments. You never know what the person next to you does for a living or what connections they might have. Of course, don't force a business conversation, and don't be salesy. After regular small talk or the first few meetups you can casually mention what you do if you think it's relevant and fits the overall context. As long as your conversation with other parents flows naturally, don't be afraid to move on to business topics.

Finally, the new experiences and new environments you encounter as a mother might inspire you to modify or redesign your business. Maybe you'll come up with a new brilliant business idea. Many women move to baby- or children-related industries once they become mothers. Some decide to work with other mothers, for example, to coach them or help them go back to work. Usually, these new businesses appear as a solution to a problem experienced by a new mother, such as lack of affordable baby-friendly and environmentally friendly toys, lack of activities for mothers in the local area, or lack of support for women who want to go back to work. By talking to other parents, you can establish whether there's a niche for your new services or if it's really worth investing in a new idea at that moment. The events, people, and surroundings of your "mothering reality" can be very inspirational for your "business reality", whether you decide to take your business in a new direction or not.

Lifelong learning

When I was at school, I always thought that real life begins once you're totally free. Free from the limits of hierarchy, boring classes, stressful tests, and unnecessary homework. I was looking forward to graduation day, but what I considered to be a completely new phase would only result in more disappointments. After the first school came another one, then yet another, then the first university, then the second and the third. While the level of freedom grew every time I progressed to the next level, my goal was always to reach the finish line that would let me define my own study and work agenda. It wasn't the studying itself that was a problem—I enjoyed and still enjoy learning new things. The main obstacle was the presence of some sort of system—grades, rules, teachers, or other people that were in charge of deciding how my education would be shaped and what subjects I was allowed to enrol in.

Once I opened my business—which I did almost immediately after graduating from university—the learning process finally became more enjoyable; free from any limitations and hierarchies. There seemed to be so many skills, strategies, tactics, and bits of knowledge that all my years at school had failed to teach me. I discovered books, online courses, blog articles, and events that were more inspiring and motivating than most of the classes I sat through in my earlier education. Real life had finally begun. I finally had the freedom to choose what I wanted to learn, how, and from whom. Now, the real challenge shifted towards finding more time to consume all these exciting resources and to implement the useful tips in my life and work. After nearly 10 years of running a freelance business, I thought I had learned so much that I could probably start teaching others how to start a freelance career or how to become a translator and localisation specialist. Then I got pregnant and the ultimate learning process began.

With all these experiences, I realised that there's no finish line that separates the process of studying from the actual doing. If you run your own business or have children, or if you're both a parent and a business owner, you need to constantly adjust, grow, enhance, and fine-tune your life. The moment you stop developing and discovering what else you could do to be a better listener, problem solver, communicator, decision maker, creator, or entrepreneur—something will suddenly surprise you and leave you breathless. Your learning process doesn't stop once you notice that you can combine your parenthood and career in a quite decent way. It doesn't stop when you eventually manage to structure your day to have enough time for your work and for your family. It continues throughout your whole life on each and every level. Keep learning and stay alert to be ready for any changes and shake-ups in your private and professional life.

The best of both worlds

Although many parents think that work-life balance is a myth, it is possible to achieve a sense of inner harmony; a state in which you're satisfied with the amount of hours you spend on your work and with the quality time you have for your family. Work-life balance will mean something different to everyone. To me, it is exactly this state of inner harmony, the awareness that I give enough energy to my family and to my business. This will probably never be a 50-50 split, and it will never be a complete balance, as that would imply that both factors are on the opposite side of a scale rather than coexisting next to each other like they do in everyday life. But it's not about splitting your day or week into equal halves.

Your business and private spheres are interdependent on many levels. For example, your work can give you a sense of worth and fulfilment that will influence the way you interact with your children and partner. On the other hand, your family, your hobbies, and routines can impact your physical and mental capability at work. Everything you do with your children is a learning experience that you can implement in your profession, and some tactics you use in your business will be a good addition to your private life. Sometimes you'll spend more time and energy on work, sometimes your focus will shift towards your family. And that's perfectly fine, as long as you give enough attention to the area that requires it the most in the given moment. In my view, this is the ultimate path towards work-life harmony.

How can you achieve this?

If you're still struggling to combine your work with other activities, it's time to redefine the idea of work-life balance. In a literal sense, such a concept would mean that work is what happens to you when you don't truly enjoy your life and that daily life shouldn't interfere with your work. Rather look at it as a work-family balance, which—although more attainable—is still difficult to accomplish. The first step to a calmer atmosphere around your work and family is to understand that there will be periods when you need to move your focus to your family and moments when you need to give more attention to your business.

Once you remember this, you can immerse yourself in the present moment by simply being mindful and concentrated on the activity at hand. When the feeling of guilt strikes and your mind drifts to your child during your work time or to your work during your family time, acknowledge this and try to actively redirect your thoughts. Instead of focusing on the reasons you should stop working and run back to your child, respond to yourself with kindness and overwrite your guilt with thoughts such as, "I am a better mother because I work," or "By working on my business I have more time for my growth, which makes me more patient and happy when I'm with my baby."

Conversely, if you feel you're wasting your time on colouring pictures of animals or building blocks with your child, reframe your guilt by focusing on why playtime is crucial for you, your baby, and your business. It can help you take a break from the hectic calls, e-mails, and meetups. It can give you an outlet for your creativity or be a great source of inspiration for your next round of work—for your marketing campaigns, your photo sessions, your designs, or your texts.

In my case, the best business ideas came to my mind when I was spending time with my family. Our activities, simple routines, or playtime offered enough space to rest, take a deep breath, and look at everything from another perspective. By fully switching to family mode, I could clear my mind and generate more energy for my next business task.

To make sure your work-family symphony is conducted skilfully, don't forget about physical activity and sufficient rest. Staying physically active will enhance your memory and learning capability, which is crucial both for your work and family. Jogging, yoga, swimming, or simple stretching exercises will also improve your mood and increase your motivation—which are critical when you have to constantly switch between your business and family. All these elements can't be complete without the proper amount of sleep to give your brain sufficient processing power and enhance your immunity and productivity.

In this way, you'll be able to keep learning and smuggling the best components of one world into the other. This is the ultimate harmony—not the amount of time you spend on work and everything else that happens when you turn off your laptop. It's how you shift your focus between different tasks and spheres while being in the moment, inspired, and ready to realign when needed.

Giving up is freeing up

The journey through motherhood and self-employment is bumpy and full of twists and ups and downs. It's not all roses and unicorns, but as long as you focus on the rewards instead of the challenges, you're on the light side of the force.

But how can you keep up your momentum and avoid going down the rabbit hole?

It's simple: you need to let something go.

Most of my interviewees share the same impression—you can't have it all at the same time. Sometimes giving up will help you free up space, time, and energy for what matters the most in a specific moment. For example, you may want to give up on your ideas and projections about being a perfect mother, perfect business owner, or a perfect business mother. Maybe, before giving birth, you visualised how patient, strong, loving, or energetic you are with your child in nearly every situation. Maybe you thought you could keep working in your office while having your child silently playing next to you on the floor. Maybe you imagined how skilfully and smoothly you could run your business for five hours per day and then happily switch to mothering mode. These are all great goals to strive for, but sometimes you'll need to lower your expectations to stay sane. Or at least postpone the deadline you set for your dreams to come true.

Give up time

Your day only has a limited number of hours. It might be difficult to accomplish everything you had planned for your business and family before you became a mother. Cramming hundreds of activities into your agenda will probably push you and your baby to the limits. If you perceive your motherhood as a long and complex project that can be broken down by thorough preparation and planning, you might end up with too many ideas and expectations that are too high. When I was pregnant, I got wildly enthusiastic about all the great things I could do with my baby. What my city offered was simply so tempting that I created a long list of activities to do, places to go, and classes to register for. But once my baby was born, my energy levels plunged. The activities list came in handy after a while and we did many amazing things, like baby swimming, mother and baby yoga, baby massage, and book readings for toddlers, but many items are still sitting on the list untouched. There are simply not enough days in a week and hours in a day to turn every inspiring idea into action.

Similarly, you might want to give up some time allocated for your business to focus more on yourself and your family. Running a business as a mother is a complex undertaking. It is definitely doable, but not without sacrifices and trade-offs. One such compromise might be related to the amount of time you spend at work. To fit in your baby and family, you might want to reduce or reorganise your business schedule. Cutting the number of hours you work, delegating, working less but with more focus—these are only some of the tactics discussed in Chapter 2 that will help you clear up more time and energy. Don't be afraid to give up on your work and hobbies if that's the only way to devote more attention to your baby. Anything you let go of now will come back to you later, maybe even in a better, reinforced form.

Give up space

You can't be everywhere and do everything, both for your business and your family. Trying to run too many projects at the same time will diminish your brain power and exhaust your energy. For example, if your goal is to bring more potential customers into your ecosystem by offering free e-books or courses, focus on one activity at a time. If you feel a constant flow of inspiration for many different aspects of your business, write everything down and go back to what you started earlier. Once you're done, revisit your ideas to see what your next move could be. Spreading yourself too thin by working on several different client attraction strategies at the same time will only slow you down. Sometimes it's better to have just one concept transformed into reality than starting on too many tasks and leaving everything halfway through. Maybe you were able to effortlessly combine marketing your business with working on paid projects before having children, but chances are that now you're a mother, your days are much shorter and more intense. Staying up the whole night to finish a project for your client because you've spent the whole day creating yet another great business promotion will kill your productivity and patience at some point. If you want to give the best of yourself to your baby, then some work-related ideas will have to stay on your to-do list for a bit longer. Focus on your priorities, and sooner or later, the right space to fit everything else will surely come.

Give up something to find yourself

You don't need to be a superwoman or a super businesswoman. There's nothing wrong with giving up on your earlier plans to find yourself and your soul. If you feel that motherhood transformed you, your energy, and your projections about your future, draft a new action plan. If you can't cope with your business anymore, try restructuring it, hiring somebody, teaming up with a colleague, putting it on hold, closing it and opening a new one, getting a coach, reading an inspirational book—there are many ways to get your energy flowing in the right direction again. If what you've been doing so far doesn't really align with your true inspiration and passion, take some steps to change your career. Give up something to find yourself again in your new role.

For example, in the first year of my motherhood, I totally gave up on marketing my services. My full attention was on my baby, and I only did paid projects, relying on my regular customers and the marketing campaigns I launched during my childless life. I used to be very active on social media and on my blog, but I put these tasks on hold when my baby arrived. Isolating myself and cutting off social media for several months probably wasn't the best approach for my business, but it was definitely the right choice for myself. Putting my business in a slower gear to embark on a soul-searching adventure helped me understand my new reality—my baby, my family, and myself. Once I came back to the social world, I felt like I was starting from scratch again. Yet, my break was inspiring and motivating. The hibernation phase helped me realise where my heart lies and in which direction I wanted to continue growing my business. This is how I came to restructure my services and create more courses, free e-books, and eventually —this book.

Giving up and taking a pause could be more inspiring than any speech you hear, any book you read, or any course you follow. All you need is to use your space and time wisely by paying more attention to what's going on inside you.

Give up to step up

What if you don't want to give up on anything at all, and you prefer to juggle work, family, children, and your hobbies? If needs be, you can quickly adapt on the go, cook with one hand, pick up a business call with another, have one eye on your baby and another on your e-mail... This method could also work out well. But it will only take you so far. If you free up one hand, maybe your meal will taste better, and if you move both of your eyes to your food, maybe it will look better too. Reduce the effort you put into several areas to give more to the one that is screaming for your attention or creates more value in the long run. This is a simple way to a more peaceful, relaxed atmosphere, both in your office and at home.

There must be something you can let go of. It doesn't have to be forever, just for a while. Maybe your intuition is already telling you want to do. Maybe there's something you simply don't enjoy doing at all—this could be a sign that it's time for wise changes. If the housework is a burden, eliminate, delegate, reduce, or restructure it. Instead of spending half of your only day off on cleaning, maybe you can divide the housework into little bits that you could complete in 20 minutes every day. Or maybe you can afford to hire someone to clean your house. Maybe your partner could be engaged in more housework responsibilities. If it's the accounting tasks that make you sick of running your business, delegate it or learn how to do it properly. If there's anything else that is stopping you from truly enjoying your motherhood or entrepreneurship, sit down and analyse all the whys, hows, and whens.

Give up on your routine, your hobbies, your actions and plans—if that's what it takes to create more space and time for your real desires. Sometimes you can only find yourself if you lose everything, or at least some things you thought you couldn't live without. It happened to me, and it happened to many other mothers too. For me, it was my morning routine that included going out at 6 am for an intensive ashtanga yoga practice, then coming home at 9 am to be able to start my day in front of the screen on a fresh and positive note. This habit was totally replaced by my baby's morning routine for many long months, but when the right time came, I got it back. And I got it back with extreme levels of inspiration, motivation, and gratitude because I realised how much I value my practice and my morning routine and how much it influences my mood, behaviour, and productivity. I also gave up on many business activities, such as networking events, but once I returned to my social life again, I knew how to make the best use of it.

You can't go back to exactly who you—and your business—were before your pregnancy, but you can move ahead by adapting your values and priorities to your new surroundings and your new identity. It's a long process, but it's definitely worth your time and energy.

Don't worry if you feel that you don't have it all figured out yet—we all doubt and struggle, we all have our ups and downs. I certainly do. On a good day, I try to look at the big picture, even if something knocks me down. On a bad day, I feel like running away from everything and hiding under a blanket. On most days, if I get caught up in what seems to be a negative experience, I keep repeating my mantra, "Everything is temporary, everything is temporary…"

Every revolution may devour its own children, but every revolution also brings new opportunities. It's only by looking inward and by focusing on one step at a time that you can control your path to a harmonious combination of work and family life.

Bibliography

This list contains books and articles that I referred to in this book or that were useful to me in the specific context of topics covered.

Books:

Ayurveda Lifestyle and Wisdom: A Complete Prescription to Optimize Your Health, Prevent Disease, and Live with Vitality and Joy, Acharya Shunya, 2017.

Chained to the Desk: A Guidebook for Workaholics, Their Partners and Children, and the Clinicians Who Treat Them, Bryan E. Robinson, 2014.

Everything is Figureoutable, Marie Forleo, 2019.

Financiën voor ZZP'ers: Weten Wat Telt!, Femke Hogema, 2012.

Food for Fitness, Anita Bean, 2007.

Macierzyństwo non-fiction, Joanna Czeczott, 2018.

Play It Away: A Workaholic's Cure for Anxiety, Charlie Hoehn, 2014.

Slowing Down to the Speed of Life: How To Create A More Peaceful, Simpler Life From the Inside Out, Richard Carlson, 2009.

The Art of Slowing Down: A Sense-Able Approach to Running Faster, Edward Yu, 2012.

The Fourth Trimester, Kimberly Ann Johnson, 2017.

The Perfectionism Workbook: Proven Strategies to End Procrastination, Accept Yourself, and Achieve Your Goals, Taylor Newendorp, 2018.

The Things You Can See Only When You Slow Down: How to be Calm in a Busy World, Haemin Sunim and Chi-Young Kim, 2018.

The Wealthy Freelancer: 12 Secrets to a Great and an Enviable Lifestyle, Steve Slaunwhite, Pete Savage and Ed Gandia, 2010.

What No One Tells You: A Guide to Your Emotions from Pregnancy to Motherhood, Alexandra Sacks and Catherine Birndorf, 2019.

Yoga Sadhana for Mothers, Sharmila Desai and Anna Wise, 2014.

Your New Pregnancy Bible, Keith A. Eddleman and Joanne Stone, 2018.

Your Pregnancy Nutrition Guide: What to Eat When You're Pregnant, Henrietta Norton, 2015.

Scientific articles:

The costs of a predictable switch between simple cognitive tasks, Rogers, R. & Monsell, S. (1995). Journal of Experimental Psychology: General, 124, 207–231.

The Maternal Brain, Kinsley C.H. & Lambert K. G. (2006). Scientific American, vol. 294, no. 1. 72–79.

Tissue microchimerism is increased during pregnancy: a human autopsy study, Rijnink, E. C., Penning M. E., Wolterbeek R. et. al. (2015) available at https://academic.oup.com/molehr/article/21/11/857/2459808 (last accessed June 2020).

Oxytocin and early parent-infant interactions: A systematic review, Scatliffe N., Casavant S., Vittner D., Cong X. (2019) available at https://www.sciencedirect.com/science/article/pii/S2352013219303229?via%3Dihub (last accessed June 2020).

Photography credits

Photo of Kateryna Vinitskyi-Sikoza by Anton Zaitseff

Photo of Anna Kamay by Julia Kochetova-Nabozhniak

Photo of Rachel by Leayshia Thompson

Photo of Magdalena Stojer-Brudnika by Anna Powierża

Photo of Mariana C. A. Passos by Mariana C. A. Passos

Photo of Anastasia Shnyper by Anastasia Suhovyi

Photo of Viki Stlema-Boviatsis by Maria Imaginária

Photo of Laura Innocenti by Laura Innocenti

Photo of Sandra Duquenne by Pierrick Deregnaucourt

Photo of Daniela Helguera by Daniela Helguera

Photo of Ambika Gupta by Berlin Flower School

Photo of Cyville Harriette F. Jaum by Pantasma Photography

Photo of Christy Racho by Lyn Ismael Bennett

Photo of Dorota Pawlak (back cover) by Yassine Ibnou-Arrahil

Found a typo?

While a lot of effort went into ensuring that this book is flawless, it is inevitable that a mistake or two will slip through the net.

If you find any errors in this book, please let me know by visiting:

www.DorotaPawlak.eu/typos

About Dorota Pawlak

Dorota Pawlak is the owner of DP Translation Services and a translator, writer, and a business consultant for freelancers. She holds an MA in Translation and MSc in Multilingual Computing and Localisation. After 10 years of freelancing and running her own business, she decided to slow down, focus on her newborn daughter, and change the focus of her business. She put a hold on her busy life as a translation course teacher, conference speaker, localisation specialist, and blogger on translation- and localisation- related topics to start helping other freelancers grow their businesses, especially other mothers who face the same challenges she did in her first year of motherhood.

Dorota regularly writes for her blog where she shares tips for freelancers and small business owners and teaches online courses at www.DorotaPawlak.eu.

Dedication

Dedicated to my mum, Anna Pawlak, my first teacher in the school of life and motherhood—for her unfailing support and positivity. She was the first person who encouraged me to develop my writing skills and the first to motivate me to open my business by running her own. She showed me that it is possible to have it all.

Thank you, Mum.

Acknowledgements

Special thanks to all the amazing women who agreed to be interviewed for this book. Without you, this book would have never happened!

Thanks to my husband, Yassine, who supported me in writing and insisted that I finally convert my ideas into reality.

Thanks to Chadia, my daughter's babysitter, for helping me create the space and time to write.

Thanks to my friend, Kateryna, who welcomed my idea with enthusiasm, kept encouraging me to publish this book, and shared her marketing ideas.

Thanks to my parents, who helped me find my parenthood style and instilled the business mindset in me.

One last thing

If you bought this book online and found value in it, I would appreciate if you could take a few seconds to rate it FIVE STARS and recommend it to your friends. If they are also business owners and mothers or mothers-to-be, they will be grateful for your recommendation.

Without stars and reviews, you probably wouldn't have found this book. Please take a moment to support an independent author by leaving a rating.

Thank you so much!

Dorota Pawlak

Printed in Great Britain
by Amazon